500 FACTS
BRITISH HISTORY

500 FACTS
BRITISH
HISTORY

Miles
KeLLY

First published in 2011 by Miles Kelly Publishing Ltd
Harding's Barn, Bardfield End Green, Thaxted, Essex, CM6 3PX, UK

Copyright © Miles Kelly Publishing Ltd 2011

The sections in this book are also available as individual titles

2 4 6 8 10 9 7 5 3 1

Publishing Director Belinda Gallagher
Creative Director Jo Cowan
Editorial Assistant Lauren White
Cover Designer Simon Lee
Designers Kayleigh Allen, Michelle Cannatella, Lousia Leitao
Indexer Jane Parker
Production Manager Elizabeth Collins
Reprographics Stephan Davis, Jennifer Hunt
Contributors Fiona Macdonald, Jeremy Smith, Philip Steele

ISBN 978-1-84810-451-8

Printed in China

British Library Cataloguing-in-Publication Data
A catalogue record for this book is available from the British Library

Made with paper from a sustainable forest

www.mileskelly.net
info@mileskelly.net

www.factsforprojects.com

Contents

THE VIKINGS 92–133

THE VICTORIANS 134–175

In the beginning

1 Human beings like us were living in Great Britain about 37,000 years ago. They hunted animals, caught fish and gathered plants they could eat. They used simple tools and weapons made of stone and wood. Britain was not an island then, but part of mainland Europe. The weather was often very cold and the land became covered in ice for long periods of time. The last of these ice ages ended about 10,000 years ago. As the weather became warmer, the ice melted and the sea level rose. Britain became an island.

▶ As the last ice age ended and the climate became warmer, bands of hunters moved into new woodlands and wetlands. As well as deer, fish and shellfish were important food sources.

Stone and bronze

▼ Animals didn't just provide meat for food. Their skins were scraped clean with flint tools and then sewn together using bone needles to make clothing and tents.

2 By 6000 BC, hunters in Britain had become skilled at making tools and weapons such as needles, fish hooks and harpoons. They hunted deer, boar and wild oxen in the oak forests. They used animal skins to make clothes and coverings for shelters.

▶ Careful chipping could turn a flint into a razor-sharp tool or weapon.

3 Flint was an excellent stone for making tools. It could be chipped and flaked until it was razor-sharp, like glass. The flints lay buried in chalk, so miners had to dig deep, as far as 10 metres down, to reach the best ones. The miners dug the flints out using deer antlers as picks.

▲ The skeletons of flint miners have been found buried in flint mines.

▲ Stone hand mills, or querns, were used for grinding wheat. The central hole was filled with grain and then the top stone was turned, or ground, against the bottom one. Flour spilled out between the stones.

4 **Farming had reached the British Isles by about 4000 BC.** Villagers learned to raise sheep and goats. They grew wheat, which they harvested with stone tools. Then they ground the grain into flour. The bread may have been gritty and the animals may have been thin and bony, but it was easier than hunting!

▶ Molten (hot, liquid) bronze could be poured into stone moulds. The mould was smeared with soot and grease to give a smooth finish. When the bronze had cooled and hardened, the mould was knocked away.

5 **Metal tools and weapons were better than stone ones.** Copper was used in Britain by 2500 BC. About 600 to 700 years later, people discovered how mixing copper with tin made a tough metal mixture, or alloy, called bronze.

I DON'T BELIEVE IT!

Some of the pillars at Stonehenge weighed as much as 20 elephants! People hauled them all the way from southwest Wales, a distance of over 215 kilometres.

6 **Between 3000 BC and 1500 BC, massive pillars of stone were used to create a circle at Stonehenge in southern England.** The stones were placed so that they lined up with the rising and setting Sun. It is thought that people used Stonehenge to study the Sun, Moon and stars, as well as to observe the seasons. People would have crowded into the circle on a midsummer morning to watch the rising of the Sun.

The ancient Celts

7 Around 600 BC, small bands of warriors and traders from mainland Europe began to settle in parts of the British Isles. Many of them belonged to a people called the Celts. Those people already living in the British Isles slowly took on the Celtic way of life. They began to speak Celtic languages, too.

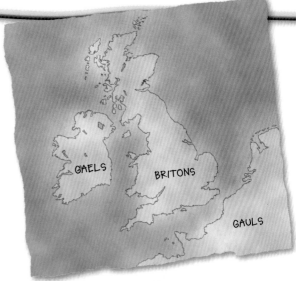

GAELS

BRITONS

GAULS

▲ The Celts gradually brought their way of life to many parts of Europe. The three main groups in the northwest of Europe were the Gauls of France, the Gaels of Ireland and the Britons of Great Britain.

8 The ancient Celts were famous for being show-offs. Celtic warriors sometimes wore their hair in spikes, tattooed their skin and wore heavy gold jewellery. Unlike most men in Europe at that time, they wore trousers beneath a short tunic. Women wore long dresses of wool or linen and used mirrors of polished bronze.

MAKE CELTIC COINS
You will need:
coins   heavy card   silver/gold paint   black felt-tip pen   scissors

1. Draw circles around modern coins onto heavy card.
2. Cut out the circles and paint them silver or gold.
3. When the paint is dry, draw your own designs with a black felt-tip pen. Celtic coins were decorated with horses, the heads of gods, or moons and stars.

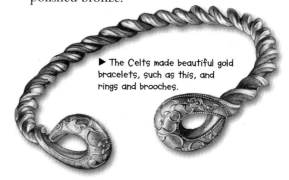

▶ The Celts made beautiful gold bracelets, such as this, and rings and brooches.

9 **The safest place to be when war broke out was on top of a hill or on a headland by the coast.** These places could easily be defended from attack with ditches and high wooden fences. Ancient Celts often used hill forts like these. The Celts were great fighters and cattle raiders. They used chariots and fought with long swords.

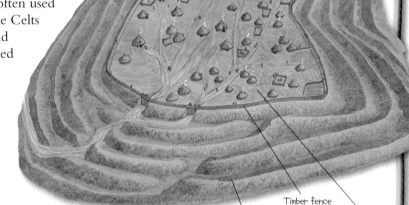

▶ This great hill fort was at Maiden Castle in Dorset, England. It was protected by timber fences and banks of earth.

Timber fence

Settlement

Bank of earth

10 **The Celts were first-rate metal workers.** They knew all about iron. In fact iron was such a hard, useful metal that people who had not seen it before thought it must be magic. Some people still nail iron horseshoes onto doors for good luck.

▶ A smoky hearth was the centre of every Celtic round house.

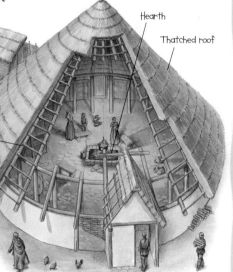

Hearth

Thatched roof

Timber poles

11 **Many British Celts lived in villages, in large round houses.** The walls were made of timber and clay, or stone. Inside each house was a fire. The smoke rose through a hole in the thatched roof. The Celts were farmers and blacksmiths and enjoyed hunting too. Their priests and lawmakers were called druids.

Roman Britain

12 **An army of 10,000 Roman soldiers landed in England in 55 BC, led by general Julius Caesar.** Despite defeating the Gauls in France, the landing was not a success and the Romans returned to Gaul. In 54 BC the Romans came back with 27,000 soldiers. They marched north to the River Thames and forced the people there to pay money to Rome.

◄ Roman coins are still found in Britain today.

13 **The Romans returned yet again in AD 43 and this time they stayed.** They conquered all of Britain except for the north of Scotland, where they built the Antonine Wall to keep the Highlanders out. In AD 122, the Roman's built Hadrian's Wall. This was the northern border of an empire that stretched from Spain, to North Africa and the Black Sea.

▲ The Roman name for Britain was Britannia. This map shows key places, roads and walls in Roman Britain.

14 **In AD 60 there was a bloody revolt against Roman rule, led by a queen called Boudicca.** She burned down Roman towns. When her warriors were defeated, she killed herself in despair. Rich Britons now learned to live like Romans. Poorer Britons carried on farming and trading, much as they always had done.

► Boudicca led her armies to war against Rome and burned down London.

15 The Romans liked their comforts.

They built public baths where people could have a cold or hot dip, a work-out or a massage. Rich people lived in luxurious country-houses called villas. These even had under-the-floor central heating.

◀ Floors were often decorated with tile pictures called mosaics.

16 Roman soldiers began to leave Britain in

AD 401. Many parts of the great empire were now under attack. In Britain there were rebellions. Pirates sailed the seas. The Irish attacked western shores. The city of Rome itself was captured by German warriors in AD 476.

17 The Romans built long, straight roads

from one town to the next. They were built using layers of sand and gravel, paved with stone. In fact, there were no better roads in Britain until the 1800s.

Stone-paved surface

Carts and horses travelled the roads

Roads were built with layers of sand and gravel

▲ Roman armies could march along the straight roads at high speed.

Anglo-Saxons

18 During the last days of the Roman Empire, raiders from northern Germany began to attack eastern Britain. More and more of them landed in the 400s and 500s. They belonged to various peoples known as Angles, Saxons, Jutes and Frisians. We call them all Anglo-Saxons. Their speech became the English language, mixed with Celtic and Latin.

▲ This Anglo-Saxon helmet dates from about AD 625.

▲ It took many years for the Anglo-Saxons to conquer much of the area now known as England. They divided it into many separate kingdoms.

▶ The Anglo-Saxons slowly conquered the southern and eastern lands of the British Celts. Armed warriors may have carried a long knife called a sax.

Sax

19 The invaders carried swords, axes and long knives. They burned down Celtic villages and old Roman towns and set up many small kingdoms. They built small villages of rectangular thatched houses and lived by farming and fishing.

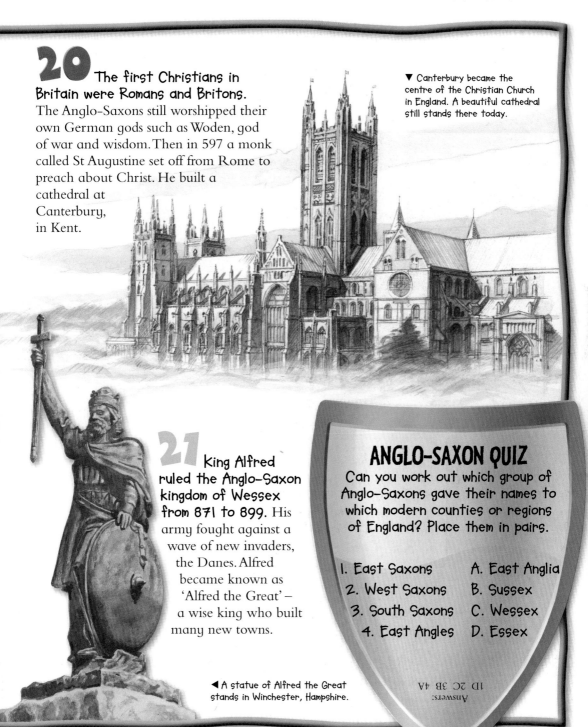

20 The first Christians in Britain were Romans and Britons. The Anglo-Saxons still worshipped their own German gods such as Woden, god of war and wisdom. Then in 597 a monk called St Augustine set off from Rome to preach about Christ. He built a cathedral at Canterbury, in Kent.

▼ Canterbury became the centre of the Christian Church in England. A beautiful cathedral still stands there today.

21 King Alfred ruled the Anglo-Saxon kingdom of Wessex from 871 to 899. His army fought against a wave of new invaders, the Danes. Alfred became known as 'Alfred the Great' – a wise king who built many new towns.

◄ A statue of Alfred the Great stands in Winchester, Hampshire.

ANGLO-SAXON QUIZ
Can you work out which group of Anglo-Saxons gave their names to which modern counties or regions of England? Place them in pairs.

1. East Saxons   A. East Anglia
2. West Saxons   B. Sussex
3. South Saxons   C. Wessex
4. East Angles   D. Essex

Answers:
1D 2C 3B 4A

17

22 **The Celtic-speaking people who lived in Ireland believed in the old Celtic gods.** Then, in about 432, a British monk called St Patrick went to Ireland to preach the Christian faith. Over the next 200 years, monasteries were founded throughout Ireland. The monks made beautiful copies of the Bible by hand.

▲ About 1200 years ago, Irish monks made books by hand. They decorated their work with beautiful letters and pictures.

MAKE AN IRISH BROOCH

You will need:

scissors   stiff card   safety pin
gold and silver paint or pens

1. Cut out a circle and a long pin shape from stiff card. Glue them together.
2. Colour one side gold with paint or a pen. Decorate with patterns as shown below.
3. Tape a safety pin on the back at the widest part of the brooch so that it can be worn.

23 **In the 700s and 800s, the Irish were some of the finest craftworkers in Europe.** They made splendid brooches and cups of gold and silver, and were also famous for their stonework. The Irish were known as great storytellers, too.

24 **In the 500s, an Irish monk called St Brendan is said to have sailed westwards to explore the lands around the Atlantic Ocean.** Tales about his voyages tell of islands, whales and volcanoes.

25 Ireland was divided into separate kingdoms. Each ruler was supposed to recognize a High King as his chief, but the kings often quarrelled and fought with each other. In about 500, one northern group of Irish set up another kingdom called Dalriada, in western Scotland.

26 Brian Ború became High King of all Ireland in 1002. He fought many battles with other Irish kings. He also fought against invaders from Scandinavia, the Vikings. Brian Ború defeated all his enemies at Clontarf in 1014, but was murdered after the battle.

◄ The Battle of Clontarf marked the end of Viking power in Ireland.

The Vikings

27 **The Vikings were pirates and raiders, traders, settlers, explorers and farmers.** Some people called them Northmen or Danes, for their homeland was in Norway, Sweden and Denmark. Viking raiders began to attack the British Isles in 789 and were soon feared far and wide.

28 **Viking longships were sleek, wooden vessels about 18 metres long.** They had a single sail and could speed through the waves. The oars were manned by a crew of 30 or more. Ships like these carried Vikings far to the west, to Iceland, Greenland and North America.

▼ The Vikings were not just interested in raiding and stealing. They realized that the British Isles provided good farmland and safe areas for settlements.

29 Viking warriors attacked monasteries, villages and towns, carrying away treasure, cattle or slaves. They were armed with round shields, axes, swords and spears and wore helmets of leather or iron. Some spent the gold they robbed buying tunics made of tough iron rings, called mail.

30 In the 840s and 850s, Viking warriors began to settle in Britain and Ireland. They lived in villages and seaports and captured large towns such as York. They founded the city of Dublin in Ireland.

31 Vikings fought against the Anglo-Saxons and soon controlled large areas of England. In 1016 England even had a Danish king called Cnut I. Vikings also ruled the Isle of Man and large areas of Scotland and Ireland.

I DON'T BELIEVE IT!

Do you know what the word berserk means? To the Vikings it meant 'bearskin shirt', as worn by warriors who worked themselves up into a frenzy before going into battle. We still use the word today to describe someone who is violently angry.

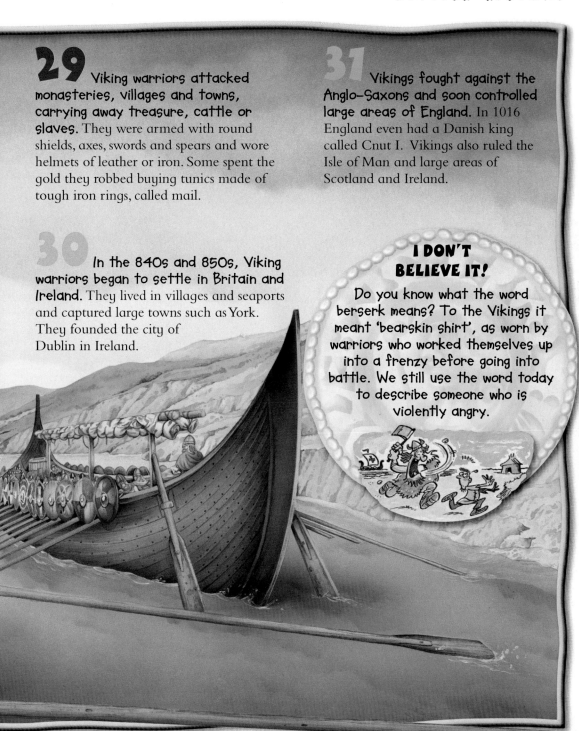

The Welsh

32 The Anglo-Saxons did not settle in the land of the West Britons, although by 607 they had cut it off from the other Celtic lands to the north. They called this land Wales. In about 784, the Saxon king, Offa, built a massive wall of earth along the border as a defence against Welsh attacks. Offa's Dyke still stands today.

◄ Crosses on early Welsh churches were beautifully carved from stone.

33 Wales and Cornwall had been centres of Christianity since Roman times. A Welsh priest called St David, who lived from 520 to 601, built new churches across the land.

► During the early Middle Ages, Wales was made up of several smaller kingdoms, each with its own ruler. These rulers were constantly fighting each other, trying to conquer the rest of Wales.

34 Wales was divided into several kingdoms. These included Gwynedd, Powys, Dyfed and Ceredigion. One ruler, Hywel the Good, ended up controlling most of Wales. He began to make new laws that were used in Wales for over 500 years. He died in 950.

Gwynedd

IRISH SEA

Powys

Ceredigion

WALES (CYMRU)

Dyfed

▲ Welsh warriors patrolled the lands to the west of Offa's Dyke. They sometimes raided parts of England for cattle and slaves.

35 Llywelyn the Great came to rule Gwynedd in 1194. He was a wise and strong ruler. He married Joan, the daughter of King John of England, but the two men became bitter enemies.

◄ This stone head is said to be a sculpture of Llywelyn the Great.

36 Llywelyn ap Gruffudd united all of Wales under his rule. He fought a long war against the English and was killed near Cilmeri in 1282. The English now ruled Wales. King Edward I declared that in future the eldest son of the English king would be the Prince of Wales.

I DON'T BELIEVE IT!

Legend says that on 1 March 640 St David was at a battle between Christian soldiers from Wales and the non-Christian Saxons. St David told his men to wear leeks in their caps to show which side they were on. The leek is still an emblem of Wales today.

The Scots

37 In about 563 an Irish monk called Columcille, or Columba, founded a monastery on the Scottish island of Iona. He travelled all over Scotland and taught people about the Christian faith.

I DON'T BELIEVE IT!

In the days before printing, people had to copy books by hand. This was mostly done by monks. It is said that St Columba copied no fewer than 300 books himself!

38 Over the years the different parts of Scotland united as one country. The Scots and Picts joined together in 847 under the rule of Kenneth MacAlpin. By 1043 all the different peoples of Scotland belonged to the new kingdom as well, which was ruled by King Duncan I.

▶ Columba arrived on the Scottish island of Iona with a handful of companions. He converted many people to the Christian faith.

39 The Scottish kings had trouble controlling their border lands. Norwegians occupied islands and coasts in the north and west until the 1100s. After them, chieftains called the Lords of the Isles ruled much of the west. Along the southern border, war with England went on for hundreds of years.

40 Duncan I only ruled Scotland for six years. He was killed by a rival called Macbeth. Macbeth actually turned out to be a good king, but in 1057 Duncan's son, Malcolm, marched back into Scotland and killed Macbeth. Malcolm became king in 1058.

◄ Duncan I became king of Scotland in 1034. He was killed in battle by Macbeth.

▶ Margaret became Queen of Scotland aged 24. She brought many good changes to the country.

41 In 1070 Malcolm III was married in Dunfermline. His bride was an English lady who had been born in Hungary. Her name was Margaret. The new queen made the Scottish court a fine place. She founded many monasteries and the Church later made her a saint.

The Normans

42 **An English king called Edward the Confessor died in 1066.** Harold II became king after him, but no fewer than seven other people claimed that they should be king instead. One of these was William, Duke of Normandy. The Normans – Northmen – were descended from Vikings who had settled in France.

43 **William crossed the English Channel with a fleet of ships.** His army landed and met the English in a great battle near Hastings in Sussex. Axes crashed on shields, arrows whistled through the air, horses neighed. King Harold was killed and the Normans marched to London.

▶ The Norman army defeated the English at the Battle of Hastings in 1066.

44 **William was crowned king of England in Westminster Abbey, London, on Christmas Day 1066.** He built a stone fortress there, as part of the Tower of London. Soon William I controlled all England. He became known as William the Conqueror.

45 The Normans created the Domesday Book. In it they recorded the houses and lands in their new kingdom. People had to work for their new Norman lords and pay taxes. The Domesday Book helped the king keep track of everything.

Domesday Book

46 The Normans attacked and settled in parts of Wales. They also settled in the Lowlands of Scotland. By 1166 Norman knights were becoming involved in wars in Ireland and seizing land there, too.

47 During the 1100s the kings of England kept close links with France. They married into French families. King Henry II of England ruled an empire that stretched all the way to southwestern France.

TRUE OR FALSE?

1. The Normans were named after their first leader, Norman the Strong.

2. The kings of England spoke French after 1066.

3. William I became known as William the Wanderer.

Answers:
1. FALSE The word Normans comes from Northmen, meaning Vikings. 2. TRUE French was the language of the royal court until the 1300s. 3. FALSE He became known as William the Conqueror.

27

Castles and knights

48 **The Normans began to build castles in Britain.** These were a type of fortress in which people lived. They helped to control areas that had been conquered. The first Norman castles were made of wood, but before long they were made with thick stone walls and had towers. Water-filled ditches called moats surrounded them. Castles were built in Britain for 400 years.

1000: a timber castle built on a mound

1150: a castle with a square stone tower, or keep

Helmet

Pauldron

Breastplate

◀ By the 1400s knights wore armour of steel plates that covered the entire body. They no longer needed shields.

Tasset

Cuisse

1300: a castle with many surrounding walls

I DON'T BELIEVE IT!

A suit of chain mail armour, as worn by a knight in the 1100s, weighed over 13 kilograms. Add to that weight the knight's great sword, axes and other weapons — and pity the poor warhorse!

49 **From the Norman period onwards, the most important troops were mounted soldiers called knights.** In battle, the knights were protected by armour. At first they wore chain mail. By the 1400s they wore plate armour that covered every part of the body, even the face.

50

Each noble family had its own badge called a coat-of-arms. This appeared on shields and flags and helped to show which knight was which during a battle. There were strict rules about the design of coats-of-arms, known as heraldry.

51

Knights liked to practise fighting in mock battles called tournaments. They showed off to the crowd and wore fancy armour. Even so, they often risked their lives.

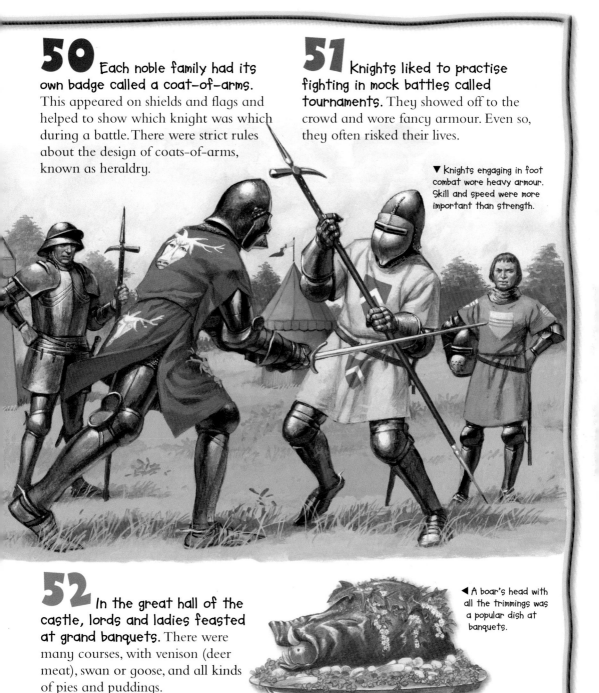

▼ Knights engaging in foot combat wore heavy armour. Skill and speed were more important than strength.

52

In the great hall of the castle, lords and ladies feasted at grand banquets. There were many courses, with venison (deer meat), swan or goose, and all kinds of pies and puddings.

◀ A boar's head with all the trimmings was a popular dish at banquets.

Life in the Middle Ages

53 **The king had power over everyone.** If the nobles served him well, he gave them land and castles. Poor peasants had to work for the local lord, providing food and fighting services in return for land. It was a hard life and sometimes the peasants revolted (rebelled) in protest.

54 **Lords sometimes revolted against the king, too.** In England, lords forced King John to sign an agreement called Magna Carta in 1215. It said that even the king had to obey the laws of the land.

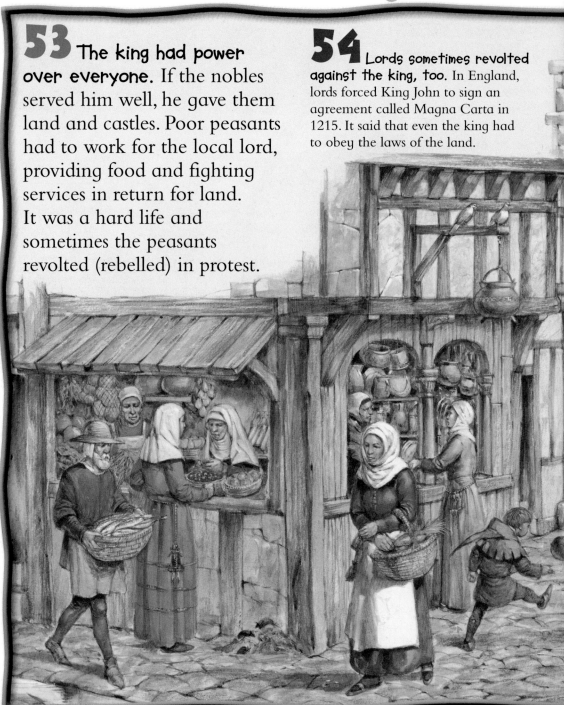

55 Towns were still quite small and were surrounded by high walls. The streets were narrow, muddy and smelly. Houses built of timber could catch fire all too easily.

56 All the Christians in western Europe now belonged to the Roman Church. Great stone cathedrals were built, soaring to the sky. People called pilgrims travelled far and wide to pray at holy sites, such as Canterbury Cathedral, in Kent.

57 In 1348 a terrible disease called the Black Death arrived in the British Isles. It was a plague that was spread by rat fleas biting people. This disease killed many millions of people right across Asia and Europe.

▼ Towns were important centres of trade and local crafts. Knights and their squires on the way to tournaments would often stop to buy food and drink.

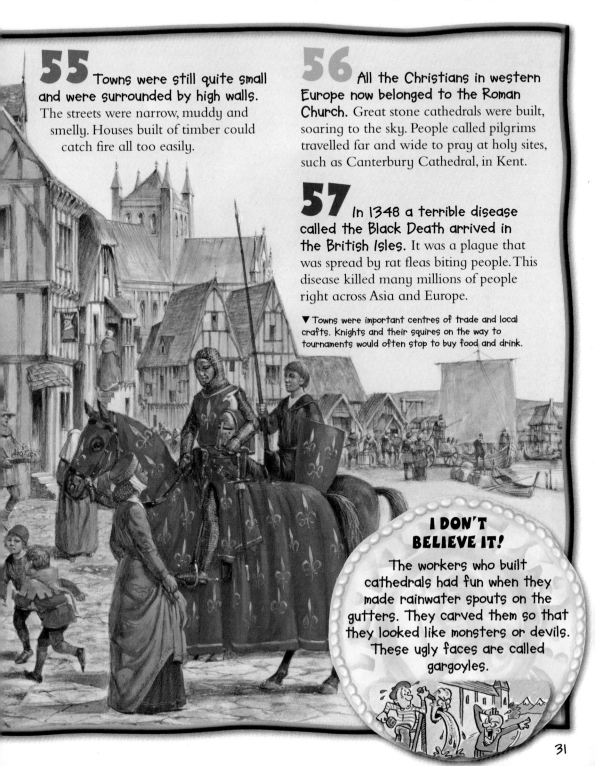

I DON'T BELIEVE IT!

The workers who built cathedrals had fun when they made rainwater spouts on the gutters. They carved them so that they looked like monsters or devils. These ugly faces are called gargoyles.

Battles and wars

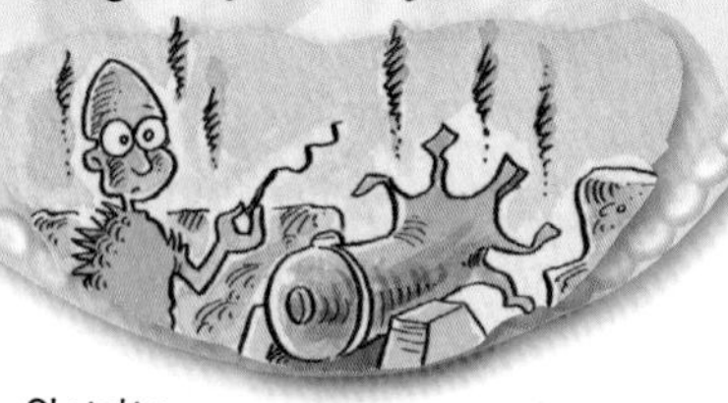

58 During the Middle Ages Christian knights from all over Europe began a terrible series of wars against people of other faiths. Most of these 'Crusades' were fought between 1096 and 1291 against Muslims in the Near East. King Richard I of England, known as *Coeur de Lion* or 'Lion Heart', led the Third Crusade in 1190.

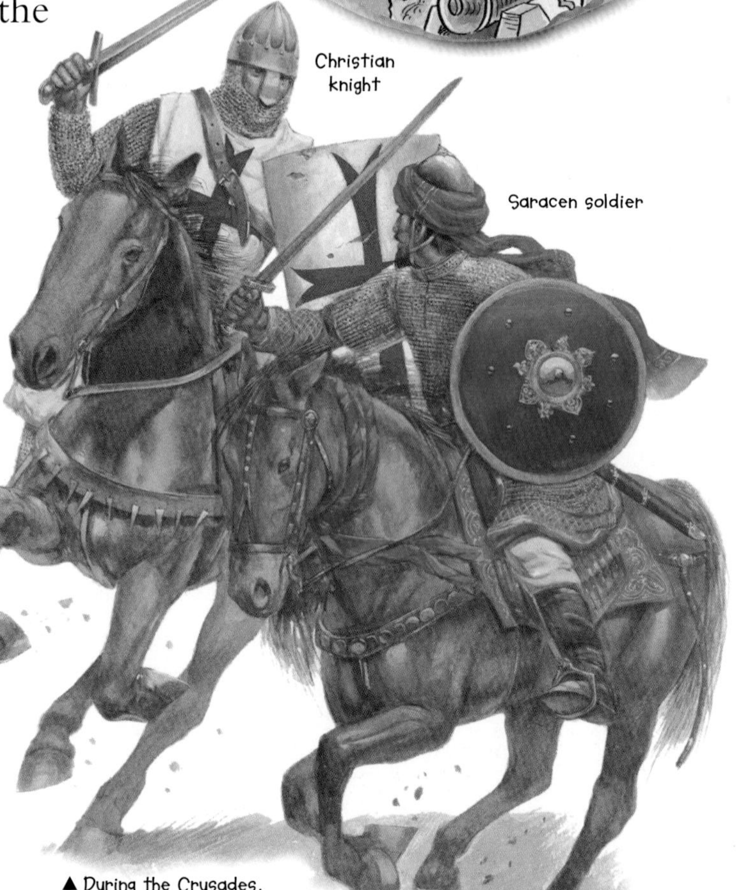

Christian knight

Saracen soldier

59 The English and Scots were deadly enemies for many years. Scottish leaders included William Wallace and Robert Bruce. Bruce often despaired of victory. One day, whilst watching a spider try and try again to rebuild its web, he vowed to do the same. He defeated the English at Bannockburn in 1314.

▲ During the Crusades, Christian knights battled with Muslim soldiers called Saracens.

60 The Welsh rose up against English rule in 1400.

Their leader was called Owain Glyndwr. He made alliances with rebel English lords and with France. Welsh archers used the new longbow, a fearsome weapon, but the rising failed after 16 years of struggle.

61 The Hundred Years War did not last 100 years!

It actually lasted longer – from 1337 to 1453. It was a series of wars between the English and the French. Henry V led the English to a great victory at Agincourt in 1415, but gradually England lost its lands in France.

English knight

Muslim archer

Scottish foot soldier

Welsh archer

62 From 1455 to 1485, two families of English nobles fought for the throne in the Wars of the Roses.

The badge of the House of Lancaster was a red rose, while the House of York had a white rose.

▲ During the Middle Ages, soldiers wore different dress for battle. They also used various weapons. The English and Welsh both favoured the deadly longbow.

The red rose of Lancaster

The white rose of York

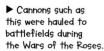

▶ Cannons such as this were hauled to battlefields during the Wars of the Roses.

33

Tudors and Stewarts

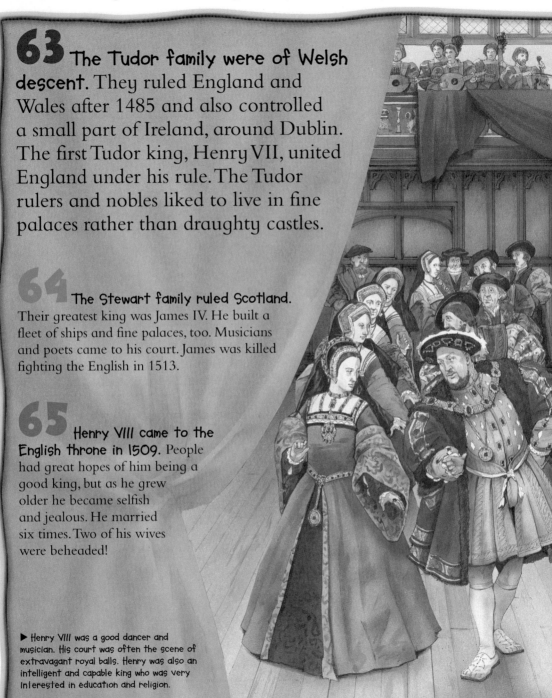

63 **The Tudor family were of Welsh descent.** They ruled England and Wales after 1485 and also controlled a small part of Ireland, around Dublin. The first Tudor king, Henry VII, united England under his rule. The Tudor rulers and nobles liked to live in fine palaces rather than draughty castles.

64 **The Stewart family ruled Scotland.** Their greatest king was James IV. He built a fleet of ships and fine palaces, too. Musicians and poets came to his court. James was killed fighting the English in 1513.

65 **Henry VIII came to the English throne in 1509.** People had great hopes of him being a good king, but as he grew older he became selfish and jealous. He married six times. Two of his wives were beheaded!

▶ Henry VIII was a good dancer and musician. His court was often the scene of extravagant royal balls. Henry was also an intelligent and capable king who was very interested in education and religion.

66 When Henry VIII tried to divorce his first wife, he quarrelled with the Pope in Rome. To get his divorce, Henry cut ties with Rome and made himself Head of the Church in England.

67 During the 1500s people were arguing about religion, in the British Isles and all over Europe. The Roman Catholics supported the Pope, but the Protestants wanted to break away from the Church in Rome. King Edward VI of England was a Protestant, but he died young. His sister, Mary I, was a Roman Catholic. In the 1550s she ordered many Protestants to be burnt alive when they refused to give up their faith.

TRUE OR FALSE?

1. Henry VIII had three of his wives beheaded.
2. Henry VIII liked to write pop songs.
3. The Stewarts changed the spelling of their name.
4. Mary I of England was a Protestant.

Answers:
1. FALSE Two were beheaded. 2. TRUE He composed all kinds of music, including religious and popular songs. He loved dancing. 3. TRUE They later spelled the name with a 'u' – Stuart. 4. FALSE She was Catholic.

The Elizabethans

68 **Elizabeth I, daughter of Henry VIII, came to the throne in 1558.** She had her father's temper as well as his love of music, dancing and fine clothes. Unlike him, she never married. She was also a much wiser ruler than Henry. Elizabeth died in 1603, the last of the Tudors.

69 **The English countryside was full of sheep in Tudor times.** Merchants sold wool and cloth across Europe. Many parts of England became very wealthy.

70 **Mary Stuart, Queen of Scots, fled to England in 1568.** Scotland was going through troubled times. Although a cousin of Elizabeth, Mary was also a threat. In 1587 she was accused of plotting against Elizabeth and she was beheaded.

◀ Elizabeth I was greatly respected, and knew how to win public approval.

▲ The smaller, faster English ships defeated the mighty Spanish fleet, or Armada.

71 English seafarers were busy exploring. In 1577 to 1581 Sir Francis Drake sailed right round the world. By the 1600s, English people were settling along the coasts of North America. Their first settlement was called Virginia.

72 In 1588 Catholic Spain sent a fleet of ships (the Armada) to invade England. The Armada was attacked by English ships along the Channel and then scattered by storms.

◀ Shakespeare's plays were first performed in the Globe Theatre during the 1600s.

73 In the 1590s and 1600s, theatres became very popular in London. People crowded into them to see the plays of William Shakespeare.

TRUE OR FALSE?

1. The Spanish Armada was defeated by the English.

2. Mary Queen of Scots became Queen of England.

3. Elizabeth I was the daughter of Henry VII.

Answers:
1. TRUE
2. FALSE She was never crowned Queen.
3. FALSE She was the daughter of Henry VIII.

Roundheads and Cavaliers

74 **Elizabeth I died without having had children.** The throne passed to James VI of Scotland, son of Mary, Queen of Scots. James now became James I of England as well. James proved to be an intelligent king who wrote about the dangers of tobacco and introduced a new English translation of the Bible.

▲ Charles I lost the Civil War and was beheaded in 1649.

75 **In 1605, soldiers searching the cellars of the Houses of Parliament discovered barrels of gunpowder.** A Catholic called Guy Fawkes along with 12 other men was accused of plotting to blow up the king and Parliament. The failure of the plot has been celebrated every 5th November since then, with bonfires and fireworks.

76 **James' son, Charles I, forced people to pay unfair taxes.** Members of Parliament were so angry that they went to war with the king. The king's soldiers were called Cavaliers and the soldiers of Parliament were called Roundheads. The Roundheads won and Charles had his head chopped off.

▼ The leaders of the Gunpowder Plot were tortured before being put to death.

77 In 1653 Parliament handed over power to a soldier called Oliver Cromwell. He ruled as Lord Protector for five years. Cromwell was supported by extreme Protestants, called Puritans.

78 In 1660 Parliament decided to have a king again. The son of the old king (Charles I) became Charles II. The Puritans took life and religion seriously and did not like dancing or the theatre. But Charles II did – people started having fun again!

▼ After the strict ways of the Puritans, people welcomed the more relaxed rule of Charles II.

I DON'T BELIEVE IT!

When he was a student at Cambridge, Oliver Cromwell was more famous as a football player than as a politician. Football was a very rough game in those days, without the rules we know today.

Plague and fire

79 **In 1665 the plague, or Black Death, returned to London.** Thousands died in the first few months. Carts came round the streets to collect the dead. City folk fled to the countryside – taking their deadly germs with them.

80 **In 1666 a spark from a fire set a bakery alight in Pudding Lane, London.** The fire spread through the city for five whole days, destroying over 13,000 timber-framed houses and St Paul's Cathedral. The city was rebuilt in stone. A new cathedral was designed by Sir Christopher Wren.

▼ Rat fleas spread the Black Death, but people did not know this. Red crosses painted on doors told people that plague was present in a house.

▼ The Great Fire of London was made worse by strong winds. About 80 percent of the old city was destroyed.

81 When Charles II died in 1685, his brother became King James II of England (James VII of Scotland). James was a Catholic and the Protestants were angry. They threw him off the throne. Instead, they made his daughter Queen Mary II. Her Protestant husband William, who already ruled the Netherlands, became king. William III and Mary II ruled jointly.

Mary II

William III

82 The 1600s and 1700s were lawless times. Highwaymen lay in wait on lonely heaths and held up travellers' coaches. Pirates sailed the seas, attacking and robbing ships.

83 Queen Anne was the last of the Stuarts. She ruled from 1701 to 1714. In 1707 it was decided that England and Scotland should have the same parliament. England, Wales and Scotland were now a United Kingdom.

◄ Highwaymen preyed upon travellers, holding up coaches and stealing valuables. Some, such as Dick Turpin (1706 to 1739), even became well-known figures.

In the 1700s

84 After Queen Anne died, the throne passed to kings from the German state of Hanover. The first four were all called George. They ruled Britain in the 1700s. By now there were two political parties called the Whigs and the Tories. From 1721 there was a prime minister, too.

86 Clever new machines were invented to spin yarn and weave cloth. They used water power or steam power. Machinery also helped on the farm. Jethro Tull invented a machine for sowing seed.

▼ Canals and new ways of farming changed the landscape of Britain in the 1700s. In fact farming changed so much, this time became known as the Agricultural Revolution.

85 Canals were built across the British Isles in the 1700s. They were dug out by gangs of workers called navigators or navvies. It was easier to carry goods on barges than on bumpy, muddy, winding roads.

87 **People called Jacobites wanted to bring back Stuart rule.** Many lived in Scotland and that was where two rebellions started. James Edward Stuart (son of James VII of Scotland/II of England) was defeated in 1715. In 1745 his son, Bonnie Prince Charlie, almost succeeded, but he was forced to flee the country after a grim defeat at Culloden in 1746.

▼ At the Battle of Culloden, the English Redcoats easily defeated the Scottish Jacobites.

The British Redcoats carried guns with bayonets (long blades attached to the end of their guns) — they attacked the Jacobites without mercy

The Scottish Jacobites wore uniforms of plaid and carried swords and shields — but they were no match for the Redcoats

Jethro Tull's seed drill

1700s QUIZ

1. What was a navvie?
2. What did Jethro Tull invent?
3. When was the Declaration of Independence drawn up?

Answers:
1. Navigator — a canal worker.
2. The seed drill. 3. 1776.

88 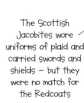 **In the 1700s British traders and soldiers were seizing land all over the world.** They fought with France to gain control of Canada and India. However in 1776, Britain began to lose control of its American colonies when the Declaration of Independence was drawn up. This recognized the right of the United States to break from British rule.

In the 1800s

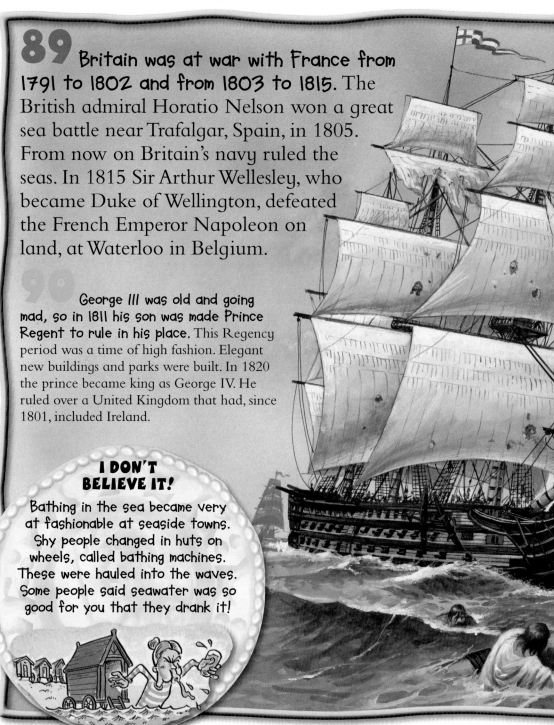

89 **Britain was at war with France from 1791 to 1802 and from 1803 to 1815.** The British admiral Horatio Nelson won a great sea battle near Trafalgar, Spain, in 1805. From now on Britain's navy ruled the seas. In 1815 Sir Arthur Wellesley, who became Duke of Wellington, defeated the French Emperor Napoleon on land, at Waterloo in Belgium.

90 **George III was old and going mad, so in 1811 his son was made Prince Regent to rule in his place.** This Regency period was a time of high fashion. Elegant new buildings and parks were built. In 1820 the prince became king as George IV. He ruled over a United Kingdom that had, since 1801, included Ireland.

I DON'T BELIEVE IT!

Bathing in the sea became very at fashionable at seaside towns. Shy people changed in huts on wheels, called bathing machines. These were hauled into the waves. Some people said seawater was so good for you that they drank it!

▼ The attempt by France to invade England failed at The Battle of Trafalgar. English cannons sank many French ships.

91 After 1804, new clanking, puffing monsters disturbed the peace of the countryside. Great Britain built the world's first railways. At first, steam locomotives were used in mines, but by the 1830s trains carried passengers.

The Victorians

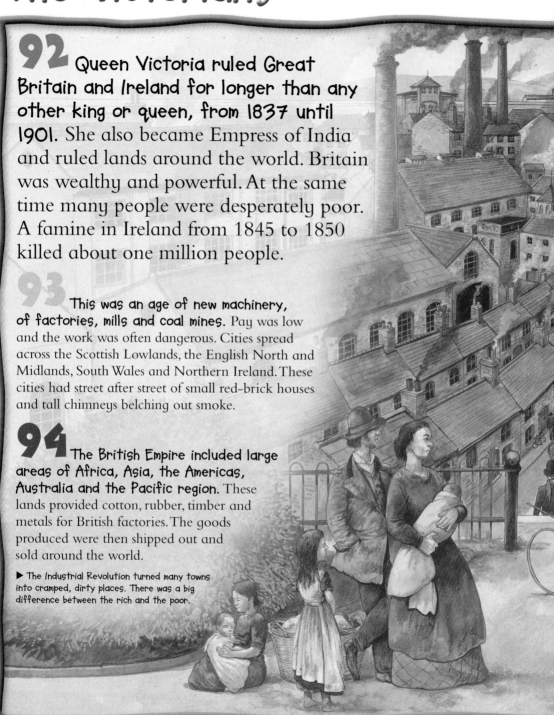

92 Queen Victoria ruled Great Britain and Ireland for longer than any other king or queen, from 1837 until 1901. She also became Empress of India and ruled lands around the world. Britain was wealthy and powerful. At the same time many people were desperately poor. A famine in Ireland from 1845 to 1850 killed about one million people.

93 This was an age of new machinery, of factories, mills and coal mines. Pay was low and the work was often dangerous. Cities spread across the Scottish Lowlands, the English North and Midlands, South Wales and Northern Ireland. These cities had street after street of small red-brick houses and tall chimneys belching out smoke.

94 The British Empire included large areas of Africa, Asia, the Americas, Australia and the Pacific region. These lands provided cotton, rubber, timber and metals for British factories. The goods produced were then shipped out and sold around the world.

▶ The Industrial Revolution turned many towns into cramped, dirty places. There was a big difference between the rich and the poor.

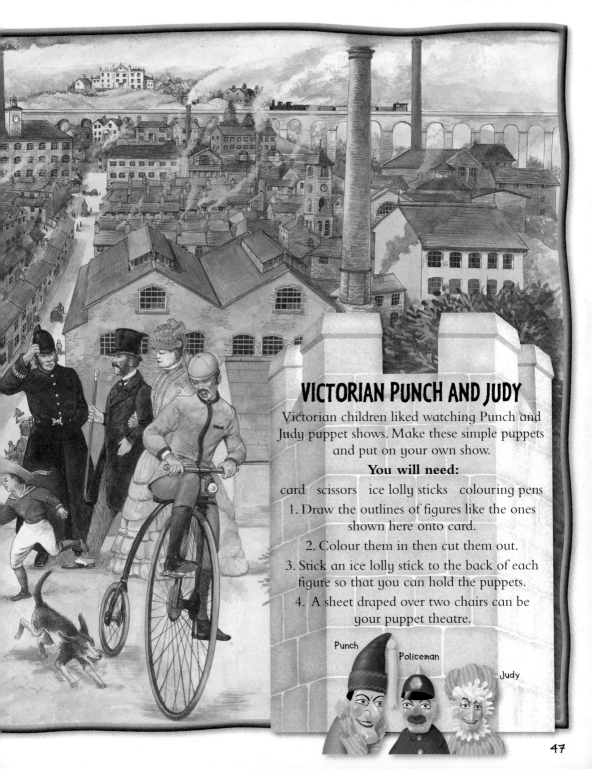

VICTORIAN PUNCH AND JUDY

Victorian children liked watching Punch and Judy puppet shows. Make these simple puppets and put on your own show.

You will need:

card   scissors   ice lolly sticks   colouring pens

1. Draw the outlines of figures like the ones shown here onto card.

2. Colour them in then cut them out.

3. Stick an ice lolly stick to the back of each figure so that you can hold the puppets.

4. A sheet draped over two chairs can be your puppet theatre.

Punch

Policeman

Judy

The modern age

95 **From 1914 to 1918 the nightmare of war spread around the world.** In Europe, soldiers fought in the mud, pounded by guns. New weapons were used such as tanks and poison gas. Ten million soldiers died in this First World War.

◀ During the First World War, the *Sopwith Camel* became the most famous British fighter plane.

96 **In 1916 there was a rising against British rule in Ireland.** In the years that followed, most of Ireland broke away from the United Kingdom and became a separate country. Across the old empire, other peoples were demanding their freedom.

97 **In the early 1900s women were marching and protesting.** Men had won the right to vote in elections. Now these women, or suffragettes, wanted to do the same. In 1918 women over 30 were given the right to vote, and in 1928 women were given the same voting terms as men.

98 **The 1920s and 1930s were a fun time for those who had money.** There were motor cars, new dance crazes and jazz records. But many people had no work – and no money. Men from the town of Jarrow walked all the way from the northeast of England to London to protest at their hardship.

◀ Hunger marchers left Jarrow for London to raise awareness of the terrible unemployment in the northeast.

99 The Second World War took place from 1939 to 1945. Britain and many other countries fought against brutal governments that had come to power in Germany, Italy and Japan. It was the worst war in history and millions of innocent people were killed. Here, British and German fighter planes chase each other during the Battle of Britain in 1940.

100 Inventions changed everyone's lives in the 20th century. This was the age of the car, the ocean liner, the aeroplane and the space rocket. It was the age of films, videos, telephones and computers. This was the modern age.

▲ The Battle of Britain began in the late summer of 1940. By October, the British had won this battle for the skies.

The Roman world

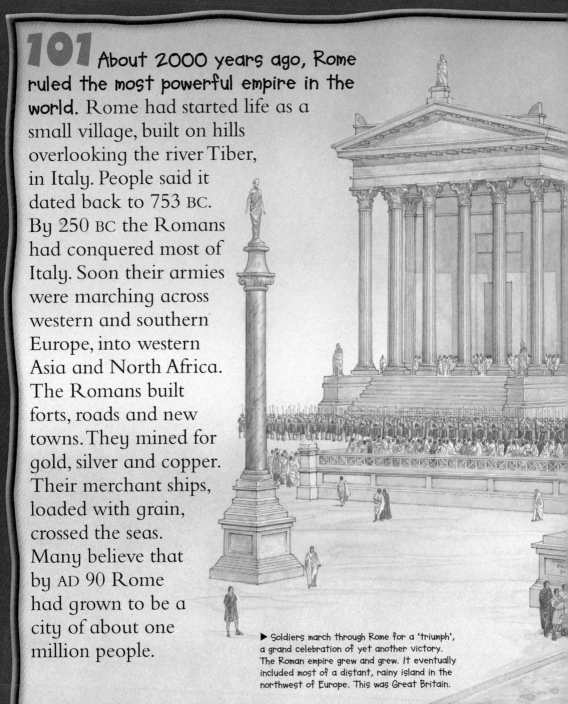

101 **About 2000 years ago, Rome ruled the most powerful empire in the world.** Rome had started life as a small village, built on hills overlooking the river Tiber, in Italy. People said it dated back to 753 BC. By 250 BC the Romans had conquered most of Italy. Soon their armies were marching across western and southern Europe, into western Asia and North Africa. The Romans built forts, roads and new towns. They mined for gold, silver and copper. Their merchant ships, loaded with grain, crossed the seas. Many believe that by AD 90 Rome had grown to be a city of about one million people.

▶ Soldiers march through Rome for a 'triumph', a grand celebration of yet another victory. The Roman empire grew and grew. It eventually included most of a distant, rainy island in the northwest of Europe. This was Great Britain.

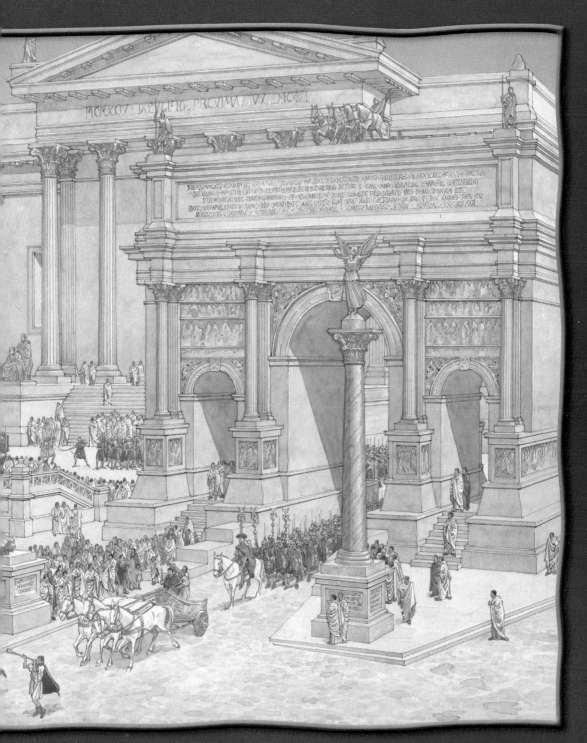

Enemies of Rome

102 **The people who lived in Great Britain in Roman times were called Britons.** Historians describe their way of life and the language they spoke as 'Celtic'. The Celtic family of peoples lived across large areas of Europe at this time, from Spain to Turkey. Other Celts included the Gaels of Ireland and the Gauls of France.

▼ This map and key show British tribes and where they lived. Some southeastern tribes, like the Catuvellauni, had arrived from the mainland of Europe as recently as about 100 BC. They were related to a tribe of Gauls called the Belgae.

CALEDONIA
(Scotland)

NORTH
SEA

IERNE
or ERIU
(Ireland)

IRISH SEA

ALBION
(Great Britain)

ENGLISH CHANNEL

1 Votadini 2 Selgovae 3 Novantae 4 Brigantes
5 Parisi 6 Deceangli 7 Cornovii 8 Ordovices
9 Dobunni 10 Coritani 11 Iceni 12 Demetae
13 Trinovantes 14 Silures 15 Catuvellauni
16 Atrebates 17 Cantiaci 18 Durotriges 19 Dumnonii

MAKE A CELTIC MIRROR

You will need:

pencil   scissors   glue stick   tin foil   gold paint   gold wrapping paper

1. Draw two circles onto card, a big one and a smaller one. Cut them out.

2. Draw the outline for the mirror handle onto card and cut it out. Glue one end to the big circle and the other end to the smaller circle (see below).

3. Paint both sides of the mirror with gold paint and allow to dry.

4. Cut out some tin foil the same size as the big circle and glue to one side of the circle.

5. Cut swirly shapes from gold wrapping paper. Glue them onto the back of your mirror as shown.

Front

Back

103 **The Britons belonged to many different tribes.** They were always fighting among themselves. Each tribe had its own king or queen and its own lands. There were important nobles, too, and priests and law-makers called druids. Most Britons were farmers and many were fine blacksmiths and iron-workers.

104
Most Britons lived in small settlements of large, round houses. These were made of timber and clay or stone, with thatched roofs. Some were built on hilltops, surrounded by fences and ditches for defence. Larger settlements or towns often surrounded royal halls.

▶ The Britons wove their clothes from linen and wool and wore cloaks fastened at the shoulder.

105
The Britons liked to wear gold jewellery. The Romans thought they were a bunch of show-offs, forever boasting about how brave they were. Women wore long dresses and the men wore tunics and trousers. No Roman man would have been seen dead in trousers!

▼ Celtic war chariots were made of wood, with iron-rimmed wheels. They carried warriors into battle.

106
Celtic warriors fought with long swords and spears and had horse-drawn chariots. In battle each warrior fought for himself. The Roman armies were very different. They were like a relentless fighting machine. Each soldier was drilled and trained to perfection.

Britons attacked

107 **In August 55 BC British warriors hurried to the cliffs near Dover as a Roman fleet approached with 10,000 soldiers on board.** Their commander, Julius Caesar, wanted to punish the British tribes because they had been supporting the Gauls who were fighting against him. The Romans sailed along the coast and then waded ashore. After a few days of fighting, a storm blew up and damaged their ships. Caesar decided to play it safe and sail home.

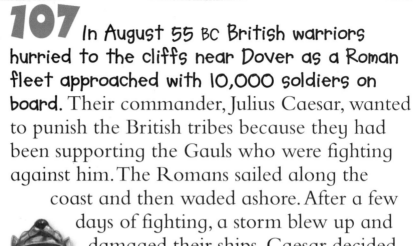

I DON'T BELIEVE IT!

When ordered to invade Britain in AD 43, the Roman troops downed weapons and went on strike. They complained that the order was unfair because the Channel shore marked the edge of the human world. Who knew what mysteries and monsters lay beyond?

◄ The first Roman into the water was the standard bearer of the Tenth Legion, or army group. The other troops leaped in and followed him to the shore.

108

Caesar returned to Britain the following summer. This time he took 800 ships, with 30,000 foot soldiers and 2000 cavalry. The troops fought their way through Kent and into Essex. At last they defeated the main alliance of tribes, which was led by Cassivellaunus, king of the Catuvellauni. Caesar made an alliance with a rival tribe called the Trinovantes and forced Cassivellaunus to pay tribute to Rome each year. Caesar left Britain after about ten weeks.

▲ The war fleet of 55 BC was much bigger than the previous invasion. It included 28 warships like this one and hundreds of other ships to carry troops, horses, weapons, equipment and stores.

◄ These coins are marked 'Cunobelin'. They show the wealth of the Catuvellauni just before the Roman conquest.

109

Julius Caesar became the most powerful man in Rome, but he was murdered in 44 BC. In the years that followed, the Romans found out more about Britain. They heard of rich prizes, such as tin mines and fields of golden wheat awaiting any invader. They sent merchants to spy out the land. They reported that the Catuvellauni were getting more powerful every day, under a new king called Cunobelinus.

110

Cunobelinus died in about AD 41. Some rival British kingdoms called for the Romans to come and teach the pushy Catuvellauni a lesson. In AD 42 the emperor Claudius put together a Roman army which was 40,000 strong. But its purpose was not just to attack one tribe. It aimed to bring the whole of Britain under Roman rule, once and for all.

Roman conquest

111 Roman troops, commanded by general Aulus Plautius, landed in Kent in spring, AD **43.** They defeated Caratacus and Togodumnus, two sons of Cunobelinus. They then fought by the river Medway and broke through massed tribes. Advancing into Essex, they captured Camulodunum (Colchester), the new capital of the Catuvellauni. It was there that the emperor Claudius, on a fortnight's visit from Rome, took the surrender of 11 tribes.

Roman soldier

Celtic warrior

▲ Celtic warriors were strong fighters. Roman soldiers were not used to their fighting techniques. It would be many years before all of Britain was securely in Roman hands.

112 Some British rulers declared their support for the Romans straight away. Indeed, some of them had already made treaties with the Romans before AD 44. Those rulers who backed the invaders did very nicely for themselves. Some were even given their own palaces, with every luxury Rome could afford. They drank good wine and had many slaves.

▶ The Romans sometimes used elephants to trample the enemy in battle. The emperor Claudius had some brought to Britain to impress the natives.

113 Many tribes tried to resist the Romans. It took about four years for the invaders to finally gain control over southern England, and another 30 years for them to conquer all of the West Country and the mountains and valleys of Wales. The battle for Yorkshire and the remainder of northern England was still underway in AD 70, when a tribe called the Brigantes rose in rebellion.

TRUE OR FALSE?

1. The Britons liked to paint themselves blue before a battle.

2. Emperor Claudius was poisoned by some mushrooms he ate.

3. The Romans invented gunpowder.

Answers:
1. TRUE A plant called woad was used to make a blue dye, which the British warriors used as war paint. 2. TRUE He died in ad 54. People believed he was murdered by his wife. 3. FALSE No, that was the Chinese, about 700 years later!

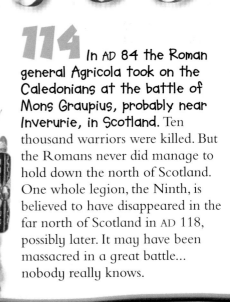

114 In AD 84 the Roman general Agricola took on the Caledonians at the battle of Mons Graupius, probably near Inverurie, in Scotland. Ten thousand warriors were killed. But the Romans never did manage to hold down the north of Scotland. One whole legion, the Ninth, is believed to have disappeared in the far north of Scotland in AD 118, possibly later. It may have been massacred in a great battle... nobody really knows.

Rebels in chains

115 **In their first summer in Britain, the Romans made a big mistake.** They let Caratacus escape. Caratacus was the son of Cunobelinus, and a cunning fighter. He and his followers joined up with tribes in Wales. From there, they launched many attacks on the Romans. Defeated at last in AD 51, Caratacus fled to the territory of the Brigantes. Their queen, Cartimandua, handed him over to the Romans. She had agreed to keep the peace with them and did not want any more trouble.

▶ Boudicca's advance was finally checked in a terrible battle. About 80,000 British warriors may have been killed and Boudicca committed suicide.

◀ After his betrayal, Caratacus and his family were taken to Rome to be paraded as prisoners of war. However, he made such a strong speech in his own defence, that the emperor Claudius pardoned him.

116 In AD 60 the Romans launched an attack on the druids (Celtic priests) because they were believed to be harbouring rebels. In AD 60 the Romans stormed the druids' sacred island of Mona (Anglesey, in North Wales). As the troops crossed the water, women screamed, warriors hurled spears and the druids called down curses. All were slaughtered by the Romans.

117 Suddenly, the Romans called off their attack on Mona and hurried away. Messengers had brought terrible news. The Iceni of East Anglia were in revolt. Their king, Prasutagus, had already made a treaty with the Romans. But when he died, Roman troops had seized his lands and assaulted his family. His wife, Boudicca, was enraged. She summoned the tribes to war. They burned down Camulodunum, Londinium (London) and Verulamium (St Albans), killing all who lived there.

I DON'T BELIEVE IT!

While the Iceni rebels were sweeping through the southeast, Roman troops had to march back from North Wales at high speed. They covered 400 kilometres in just 14 days – and faced new battles when they got there. The cavalry raced ahead of them.

Britannia!

118 Britain was now 'Britannia', a province of the mighty Roman empire, with its capital at Londinium. It was ruled by a governor. The province was divided into territories, military settlements and towns. Each had a council and elected magistrates to enforce the law.

◄ This coin from AD 150 shows the figure of a woman with a spear and shield as an emblem of Britannia.

119 The Roman army kept strict control over Britannia. They set up military camps during the conquest, and soon replaced their leather tents with strong forts built of timber and then of stone. These could cover 20 hectares of land. They had barracks, officers' headquarters, parade grounds, grain stores, workshops, hospitals, baths and toilets, too. Often a village or a town would grow up outside the walls of the fort as well.

▲ Roman forts were built and repaired by the troops themselves. The everyday work of a soldier involved carpentry, construction and engineering as much as fighting battles.

▲ Ruins like this help us understand how the Britons lived under Roman rule. The site in Wales has the remains of stone huts, grain stores and walls. It probably belonged to a local chieftain.

PLACE NAME DETECTIVE

The Roman word for a camp or a fort was CASTRUM. Any places in modern Britain ending –CASTER or –CHESTER were probably once military centres of the Roman occupation. Can you think of any near you? If not, check any road map of Britain.

120 **During the conquest, many Britons had been killed in battle or enslaved.** But as the years went by, more and more Britons in the towns took on Roman customs. Even so, in more remo countryside the old Celtic way of life continued much the same as before, hunting, herding cattle or sowing crops.

▼ A travelling merchant shows jewellery to a wealthy Roman lady. She needs a new necklace for the governor's dinner party.

121 **Soon there were quite a few Romans living in Britannia.** There were young officers newly arrived from Rome, upper-class ladies, children, doctors, shopkeepers and servants. Many Roman soldiers settled in British towns when they left the army, sometimes taking a local wife. Not all the newcomers came from Italy. Soldiers, merchants and slaves arrived from all over the Roman empire – including Germany, Greece, Spain and North Africa.

Marching with the Eagles

122 The Roman army was divided into legions of about 3000 to 5000 men. Each legion had its own battle standards, tall poles topped with an emblem such as an aquila – an eagle of gold. Legions were divided into smaller groups called cohorts and centuries. Other army groups called auxiliaries provided support. These were made up of troops who were not Roman citizens.

123 A soldier in a legion was expected to serve for 25 years. Each new recruit was given long hours of marching, weapons-training and drilling. On active service he had to carry his own weapons, armour, tools and rations such as hard biscuits, cheese and sour wine.

124 A legionary in the early days of the conquest wore a helmet of iron or bronze with cheek guards and a flap to protect the neck. Caesar's troops wore shirts of iron mail, but by the AD 100s, armour made of metal plates was being strapped over the soldier's tunic. A new type of shield was being carried by then, too. It was rectangular and curved and made from wood and leather.

125 The legionary was armed with a javelin and a short sword. Cavalry carried a longer sword. Slings and a variety of spears or daggers were also used in battle. Auxiliaries from Asia were often used as archers, armed with bows and arrows.

126 When they stormed a Celtic hill fort, Roman troops would often form a 'tortoise'. This formation was created by soldiers lifting their shields above their heads. Spears and rocks would bounce off the tortoise's 'shell'.

QUIZ

1. When were Roman soldiers allowed to marry?
a. Any time b. After 10 years' service c. On retirement

2. Who first used saddles on horses?
a. Celts b. Romans c. Germans

3. How long was a Roman soldier expected to serve?
a. 5 years b. 15 years c. 25 years

Answers:
1C 2A 3C

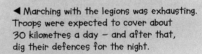

◄ Marching with the legions was exhausting. Troops were expected to cover about 30 kilometres a day – and after that, dig their defences for the night.

127 Giant catapults were used to hurl arrows or pointed missiles called bolts at the enemy. Round stones and heavy boulders were hurled by a machine called a ballista. The strong timber gates of a hillfort could be destroyed by a battering ram or by fire, as happened in AD 43 at Maiden Castle in Dorset.

63

Frontier defence

128 Great Britain formed the northwestern frontier of the Roman empire. The Romans never conquered Ireland, so most of the frontier followed the coastline. In the north of Britain, however, it crossed the land, and was defended by a wall.

▲ Hadrian's Wall became the permanent frontier. From Bowness in the west and Wallsend in the east, there were 15 larger forts.

129 The emperor Hadrian gave his name to the great northern wall, which was begun in AD 122. It ran for 117 kilometres, from the Solway Firth to the river Tyne. Its aim was to keep out the tribes on the northern side and to prevent them from making alliances with tribes on the southern side. The wall made it easier to move troops and supplies.

▶ A Roman patrol brings in two Picts ('painted people') from beyond the wall, for questioning.

130
Hadrian's Wall was built of stone, about 4 metres high by 3 metres wide. It was defended by ditches and at every Roman mile (1500 metres) there was a mini-fort with a tower to guard crossing points. There was a string of larger forts along the wall, and the large Vindolanda base (Chesterholm) was built on an east-west road to the south of the wall.

131
Serving on Hadrian's Wall must have been boring for the auxiliary soldiers – Romans, Gauls, Dutch, Germans and other defenders of the empire. When the troops weren't building and digging, they had marches, weapons-training or drill on the parade ground. In their spare time they hunted, gambled, drank wine or beer, or wrote letters home. Many documents have survived, such as accounts books, requests for leave, even a birthday invitation from an officer's wife to her friend.

132
Twenty years after Hadrian's Wall was started, the Romans built another wall across the Scottish Lowlands, between the Firth of Forth and the river Clyde. The Antonine Wall was a great bank of soil built over cobble stones. It never became a permanent frontier.

133
Coastal defences were built in places where there was risk of attack. Saxon raiders from mainland Europe crossed the North Sea and the Channel. From about AD 280 onwards, eastern and southern coasts, known as the 'Saxon shore', were defended by castle-like forts and stone walls.

A network of roads

134 The Romans introduced the first planned system of roads in Britain. Some were minor routes but others were up to 12 metres wide, straight and well-drained. The chief aim of these roads was to allow the legions to march quickly from one part of the country to another. No better roads were built until the 1800s.

135 Roads were made using whichever stone was available locally. The route was carefully surveyed and forest was cleared well back from the verges, to prevent ambush. Layers of broken flint and crushed stone were laid as foundations. The surface was generally of gravel, but sometimes paved. The roads were built by the army using troops, or slaves as labour.

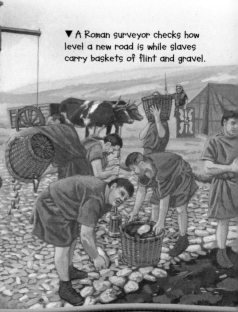

▲ Stone pillars (milestones) were erected to show distances between towns in Roman miles. Many of them showed which emperor was ruling at the time. This milestone bears the name Victorinus, who came to power in AD 269.

▼ A Roman surveyor checks how level a new road is while slaves carry baskets of flint and gravel.

136

The Roman road network was centred upon Londinium (London). From there, main roads went out to the chief army towns – Dubris (Dover), Camulodunum (Colchester), Noviomagus (Chichester), Isca Dumnoniorum (Exeter), Viroconium (Wroxeter) and Eboracum (York). A cross-country route from Exeter to Lindum (Lincoln) marked the temporary frontier of the advancing Romans in AD 47. Some sections of these routes still carry traffic today.

QUIZ

1. How far could a Roman soldier march in one day?
   a. 10 kilometres b. 20 kilometres
   c. 50 kilometres
2. How many kilometres of road did the Romans build in Britannia?
   a. 900 b. 4000 c. 9000
3. Who repaired roads and bridges? a. local councils
   b. slaves c. local farmers

Answers:
1C 2C 3A

137

The most important travellers on the roads were the official messengers, who rode on horseback. They travelled at speed, obtaining fresh horses from wayside inns. Some travellers used fast, lightweight carts pulled by mules, while others rode in slower, horse-drawn carriages. Heavy goods were carried in wooden wagons hauled by teams of oxen.

▼ Slow traffic would move onto the broad verges to let a courier or cavalry unit ride down the central roadway at speed.

Ox-cart

Mule cart

Official courier on horseback

Roman towns

138 The Romans built towns, often on the sites of the former tribal capitals of the Britons. Smaller towns and villages grew up around crossroads, along rivers and by the sea. The Romans who moved into these towns were officials, lawyers, traders or craftworkers. They were soon joined by those Britons who could afford to take up the Roman way of life.

139 The Roman period saw the first proper towns in Britain. They had paved streets with houses laid out according to a grid plan, market places, temples, statues, public baths, shops and workshops. Major towns or cities were surrounded by defensive walls.

140 Londinium (London) was sited on the banks of the river Thames. It was ideally sited for trade with the rest of the empire. A long, wooden bridge was built across the river. London became a great centre of trade and was the biggest city in the province. At its peak it had a population of about 45,000. An army fort was built, a huge town hall, or basilica, a market place or forum and temples.

141 Townhouses were built of timber, and later stone and brick.

Shopkeepers and craftworkers mostly lived on the premises behind their shopfronts. Some houses had six or more rooms and were quite grand, with painted walls, tiled floors, courtyards and gardens.

142 The Romans were great engineers.

Their towns were supplied with fresh water by aqueducts (water channels) and pipes made of lead and timber. Towns had drains and sewers.

▲ The biggest towns in Britannia, such as Londinium, served as military bases.

Temples and shrines

143 **The Romans believed in many gods and goddesses.** There was all-powerful Jupiter, Venus the goddess of love, Mercury the messenger of the gods, Diana the goddess of hunting and Saturn the god of farming. Every Roman knew old stories about the gods. In these, the gods behaved very much like humans, quarrelling and falling in love.

▲ A statue of Jupiter, king of the Roman gods. Images of the gods were placed in temples and public places.

144 Some Roman temples were built in stone, often with splendid pillars and painted walls. At the centre was a sanctuary or shrine. People might make offerings or give thanks to the gods, but there was no public worship.

▲ The great temple of Claudius at Colchester was one of the first in Britannia. It was built to impress the Britons, but was destroyed by Boudicca. It had to be rebuilt after her rebellion was crushed.

145

Some Roman emperors were officially worshipped as gods. It helped them keep control over the people, if they could claim to be super-human. A great temple to the emperor Claudius was built at Colchester. He was a lame, stammering man, who was very clever. He must have smiled to himself at the thought of being honoured as a god.

TRUE OR FALSE?

1. January is named after Janus, the Roman god of doorways.
2. The Romans made human sacrifices to their gods.
3. Many of the planets are named after Roman gods.

Answers:
1. TRUE Janus was shown with two faces, one looking backwards and one looking forwards. 2. FALSE Animals were sacrificed to some of the gods. 3. TRUE We have named all the planets except Earth after Roman gods and goddesses.

▲ Mithras, the Persian god of light, was often shown slaying a bull.

146

All sorts of foreign religions became popular in Britannia over the years. Isis was an ancient Egyptian goddess who gained many followers. Mithras, the Persian god of light, was very popular with the troops. Many temples were built to honour Mithras, including one in London.

147

In the countryside, the Britons still worshipped the old Celtic gods and goddesses. Many of the Roman newcomers happily adopted these gods, too. They identified them with similar Roman gods and built temples and local shrines to a lot of them.

◀ This statue honours a tribal goddess called Brigantia, who was reckoned to be the same as the Roman goddess of wisdom, Minerva.

Villas in the country

148 **Villas were large Roman country houses.** They were normally built at the centre of a large estate, with orchards and fields of wheat, flocks of sheep or herds of cattle. Labour was provided by slaves. Villa owners were often the wealthier Romans, such as government officials or retired army officers. Many Britons also became landowners in the Roman style.

149 **Over the years, villa design became more and more luxurious.** The buildings had dining rooms, kitchens, bedrooms, bathrooms and courtyards. They even had central heating. Warm air from a furnace passed along channels under the floor and then up a flue behind the walls.

▼ Country villas were owned mainly by the rich. The first villas were simple farmhouses but as Rome prospered, villas became magnificent mansions built all over the empire. Walls were covered with paintings and beautiful mosaics decorated the floors.

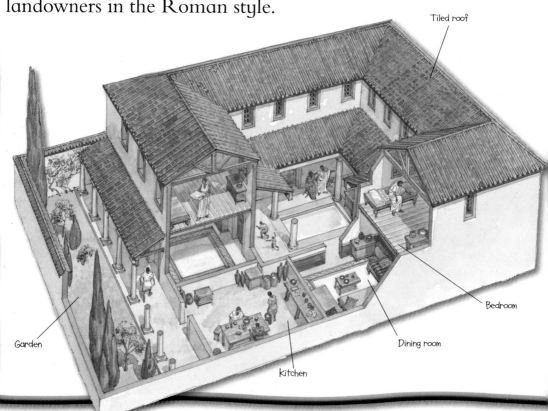

Tiled roof

Bedroom

Dining room

Kitchen

Garden

150

Floors were decorated with mosaics. Mosaics are pictures built up from thousands of small tiles made from coloured stone or pottery, set in cement. Some featured patterns, others showed images of gods, seasons, animals or fruit. Craftsmen would travel from one site to another to lay new floors.

▲ This mosaic may have been designed for the floor of a bathhouse.

MAKE A ROMAN MOSAIC

You will need:

card   pencil
coloured paper   glue

1. Take an A3-size sheet of card.

2. Draw the outlines of your picture or pattern.

3. Cut or tear paper of various colours into fragments about one centimetre square.

4. Glue them to the card, building up the picture within the outlines you have drawn.

151

Houses and gardens were often decorated with statues. Stone carvers also produced shrines to the gods who were believed to protect the household from harm.

152

The estates also offered hunting with dogs. Deer were a popular choice of prey as venison was a welcome addition to the menu at dinner time. Boar (wild pig) was common in Britain and was a fierce animal when cornered by hunters with nets and spears.

▶ A charging boar could send a hunter flying and its sharp tusks could gash a leg badly.

Working the land

153 **The estates of the new villas might cover an area of 500 to 1000 hectares.** They were often sited on the best farmland. Farming methods began to improve. The Romans dug new wells. They raised cattle, sheep, pigs, goats, ducks and geese by breeding from the best stock. They built new ovens for drying grain before threshing, a useful invention in Britain's damp climate.

▲ Fruit trees were planted around many Roman villas in Britain and were carefully tended through the seasons.

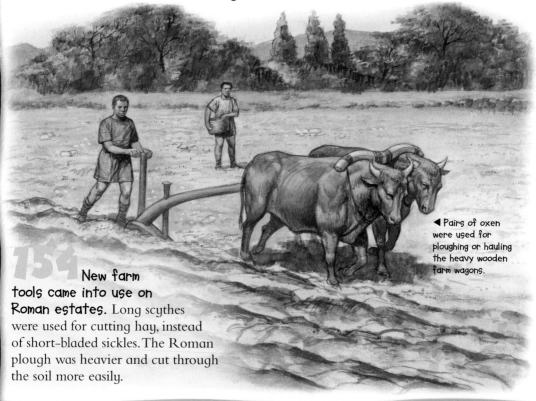

◀ Pairs of oxen were used for ploughing or hauling the heavy wooden farm wagons.

154 **New farm tools came into use on Roman estates.** Long scythes were used for cutting hay, instead of short-bladed sickles. The Roman plough was heavier and cut through the soil more easily.

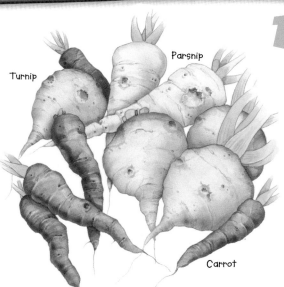

Turnip

Parsnip

Carrot

155 The Romans brought crops that had been unknown to the Britons. They grew rye, oats and new root and leaf crops such as cabbages, carrots, parsnips and turnips. Roman estate managers planted the first plum and walnut trees and they tried growing grape vines in the more sheltered, southern regions of Britain.

◄ Vegetables grown in Roman Britain included carrots, turnips and parsnips.

156 Retired Roman soldiers who settled in Britannia used to grow vegetables on small plots by their home. They might keep ducks on the pond or pottery hives full of busy bees. Bees were valued very highly, for honey was the only food sweetener in the days before sugar was used.

157 Large areas of Britain were still farmed by Britons who had not adopted Roman ways. These smaller farms surrounded traditional thatched dwellings, often in the more remote, highland areas of Britain. The farmers herded sheep and cattle and grew barley and a type of wheat called spelt.

TRUE OR FALSE?

1. The Romans built ovens for drying grain before threshing.
2. Cattle were used for ploughing.
3. The Romans planted the first plum trees.

Answers:
1.TRUE This was a useful Roman invention. 2. FALSE Oxen were used for ploughing. 3.TRUE The Romans planted the first plum and walnut trees.

Fair trade

158 Romans arriving in Britain missed the food and drink they were used to at home. They had them imported by ship. Such items included decent wine, olive oil from the Mediterranean and a kind of fish sauce that the Romans loved to cook with. They also imported glass and pottery, at least until local workers learned to produce quality goods.

159 British goods shipped abroad included wool, often in the form of cloaks for winter, and woollen rugs. The hold of a merchant ship might be filled with British grain or minerals, salted fish or live oysters. British hunting dogs fetched a good price on the other side of the Channel.

160 The merchant vessels that sailed around British coasts were very different from the streamlined warships. They were wooden, with big steering oars at the rear and a single sail. Goods were shipped in sacks and crates, while wine or oil was transported in large pottery jars.

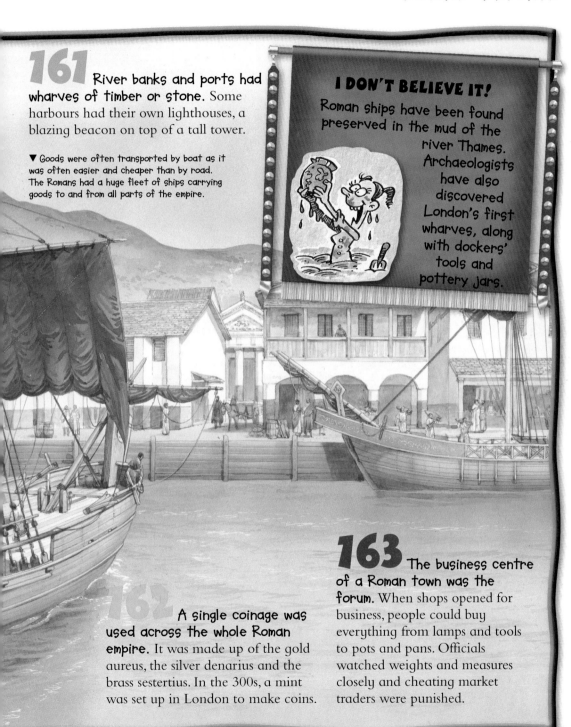

161 River banks and ports had wharves of timber or stone. Some harbours had their own lighthouses, a blazing beacon on top of a tall tower.

▼ Goods were often transported by boat as it was often easier and cheaper than by road. The Romans had a huge fleet of ships carrying goods to and from all parts of the empire.

I DON'T BELIEVE IT!

Roman ships have been found preserved in the mud of the river Thames. Archaeologists have also discovered London's first wharves, along with dockers' tools and pottery jars.

162 A single coinage was used across the whole Roman empire. It was made up of the gold aureus, the silver denarius and the brass sestertius. In the 300s, a mint was set up in London to make coins.

163 The business centre of a Roman town was the forum. When shops opened for business, people could buy everything from lamps and tools to pots and pans. Officials watched weights and measures closely and cheating market traders were punished.

A hard day's work

164 The Britons had made good pottery long before the arrival of the Romans. However, under Roman rule, pottery-making became a big industry. The design of the kilns in which pottery was fired and hardened was improved. Dishes, jugs and kitchenware were turned out on a large scale. Many showing the maker's trademark have survived.

▲ Potteries grew up wherever there was good clay, many in Oxfordshire and southern England. The town of Durovernum Cantiacorum (Canterbury, in Kent) was a centre of glass-making.

▼ The Romans had no spinning wheels. Instead, a spindle such as this was twirled around. It stretched and twisted the woollen fibre into yarn for weaving.

165 Weaving, too, became a big industry under the Romans. Work was usually done by poorer women. The wool was still spun into yarn at home, using a hand-held spindle. The weaving and finishing of the cloth was now often carried out in larger workshops, or mills.

166 The Romans hoped that Britain's minerals would make them rich. The miners were mostly slaves and led wretched lives. They mined for gold and copper in Wales, tin in Cornwall, coal in the northeast, iron in the southeast and Midlands, lead in the West Country and Derbyshire. They could get silver from the lead by heating it to a very high temperature.

167 The Romans could teach the Celts little about ironworking and blacksmithing. That was their speciality. Business boomed and there were always red-hot axes, pans or horseshoes to be beaten out with the hammer.

▲ The forge was at the centre of every village and town. More and more iron goods were being made and repaired in Roman times.

168 As the Romans settled in Britannia, they needed stone to build new towns, bridges, aqueducts and temples. Quarries were worked all over the country. Rock was heated with fire until it cracked, then levered away in slabs and cut into blocks.

QUIZ

Can you give each Roman or British worker the right tool for the job?

1. Stonemason
2. Sailor
3. Potter
4. Blacksmith
5. Weaver

a. Anchor
b. Loom
c. Wheel
d. Chisel
e. Anvil

Answers:
1d 2a 3c 4e 5b

Learning and medicine

169 The children of wealthier Britons and Romans living in towns went to school at age six to seven. Here they would learn reading, writing, history, sports and arithmetic. Most children left school at the age of 11 and might have continued with their education at home.

171 The Romans had various ways of writing. They could scratch letters onto a wooden tablet covered in wax, using a sharp point called a stylus. Important documents were written with pen and ink on parchment (prepared animal hide) or papyrus (a type of paper made from reeds). School children practised writing on broken pottery.

◄ A tutor teaches his pupils how to recognize the letters on a scroll of parchment. Lessons tended to be dull and tutors often hit the children if they got the answers wrong.

170 Girls might be expected to learn weaving and some were given lessons in playing an instrument called the lyre. Girls from important families might be taught the same lessons as the boys. All girls were expected to learn how to run a household, as a training for married life.

172 Arithmetic for beginners involved much counting with the fingers of both hands. Instead of calculators, Roman children used a counting frame, or abacus. They pushed counters along the rows to work out sums.

Abacus

▼ Roman surgeons used many instruments for operations

Spoons were used for giving medicine

Forceps helped to remove spearheads from soldiers' wounds

Hooks held wounds open during operations

Ointment was applied with a spatula

174 Science and medicine were still quite basic and few people lived to see old age. There were many herbal medicines and potions and some of these did work. Doctors dealt with eye infections and surgeons carried out all sorts of operations. Poppy juice and wine were used as anaesthetics (pain relievers).

173 The Britons in the countryside spoke a Celtic language known as Brythonic. This later developed into the Welsh, Breton and Cornish languages. The Romans in the towns spoke Latin, and soon any Briton who wanted to get on in life had to learn it too. Latin remained the language of the Church, the law and universities long after Roman rule of Britain had come to an end.

Let's speak LATIN!

Here are some of the Latin words that the Britons had to learn.

boy	puer	(POO-er)
girl	puella	(poo-ELL-a)
British	Britannicus	(brit-ANN-i-coos)
soldier	miles	(MEE-lays)
sea	mare	(MAH-ray)
island	insula	(IN-soo-lah)
horse	equus	(ec-WUSS)

175 Every Roman town had to have its public baths. Even the better-off British enjoyed bathing too, while the job of the slaves was to stoke the furnace that heated the water. The bath house was the noisiest building in town, echoing with the sound of splashing water and chatter. Men and women bathed separately. They went there to get clean, to relax, to have a massage or a work-out or to gossip with friends. One of the most popular Roman baths was at Aquae Sulis (Bath).

I DON'T BELIEVE IT!

Chariot-racers had the same following of fans as the football stars of today. Everyone knew their names and nicknames and followed their favourite team, such as the reds or the greens.

176 At Isca Silurum (Caerleon, in South Wales) crowds watched gladiators fight. Gladiators were slaves or prisoners who were given a chance to win popularity or freedom in public combat. They often fought to the death. Other entertainments included boxing and chariot-racing. Amphitheatres in Britannia were not as grand as those in Rome.

177

Any fair-sized town had its own open-air theatre. Rows of wooden seats, set into a bank of earth, rose in a half circle around the stage. The show might include dancing, music, plays about Roman gods and goddesses, and comic sketches. Groups of actors probably toured Britannia, travelling from one town to another.

▼ The baths at Aquae Sulis (Bath) had changing rooms and lockers, hot baths, warm baths and cold baths — but no soap. Bathers oiled their bodies and then scraped themselves clean.

179

Children's toys included marbles, dolls and toy chariots. Roman and British children must have swum in the rivers in summer, raced each other round the houses and played different ball games.

178

The Romans loved playing games and gambling. The clatter of rolling dice could be heard in bath houses, inns and barrack rooms around Britannia. Favourite games were called 'Tables', 'Robbers' and 'Three Stones' (which was a version of noughts-and-crosses). A popular girls' game was tossing little bones into the air and seeing how many they could catch on the back of the hand.

▼ Boards made of pottery and little gaming pieces of bone, glass, clay or ivory have have been dug up at Londinium (London) and Calleva Atrebatum (Silchester).

Togas and jewels

180 The most common Roman dress was a simple, practical tunic, which was worn by working people, slaves and children. A woollen cloak was worn for warmth. Important men wore a white robe called a toga. It looked good, but it was bulky and uncomfortable to wear. Men of high rank wore togas with a purple trim.

▼ ▶ Roman ladies wore fine jewellery, some of it made locally.

Gold earrings

Jet bangle

Gold ring

181 Most boys and girls wore togas like their parents. Married women wore a coloured dress called a stola and a shawl called a palla, which could be draped over the head and shoulders.

▼ At the height of the empire, women wore a brightly coloured robe called a stola and a shawl known as palla. Children wore knee-length tunics. Men too, took an interest in fashion, and wealthy families wore only the finest cloths.

182 Like today, hairstyles went in and out of fashion. At the time Hadrian's Wall was being built, Roman men were cleanshaven. Later it was fashionable for them to grow beards. Women would curl, plait or pin up their hair. Wigs and hair extensions were popular, as were headdresses and hairbands. Make-up included lipstick, eyeshadow and a white face powder made from chalk or even poisonous lead. Perfumes and scented oils were kept in beautiful little bottles and jars.

Necklace set
with jewels

185 Working clothes included wrappings of cloth worn as leggings and hoods to keep out the cold. Leather cloaks were waterproof against the British rain.

MAKE A ROMAN PENDANT

You will need:
scissors   thread or wool   card
paint   paintbrush

1. For the chain, cut the thread or wool to the right length for your own neck.

2. For the pendant, cut out a disc of card.

3. Paint a design on the card. It could be a dolphin or perhaps a scary monster called a gorgon, with a woman's face but tangled hair full of snakes.

4. Make a hole near the top of the disc and thread the 'chain' through it.

183 Men and women wore rings of gold, silver or bronze. Many of these were set with amber or precious stones. Rich women wore necklaces and earrings of gold and pearls, while poorer women made do with beads of glass or ceramics. In Yorkshire the shiny black stone known as jet (a sort of fossilized wood) was carved into bangles and beads. Cloaks were fastened with fine brooches.

184 Romans wore leather sandals on their feet. Even soldiers wore these, with studded soles so that they were not worn out by marching. Leather shoes, too, have been found in London. Boots were worn for riding or for muddy, winter days.

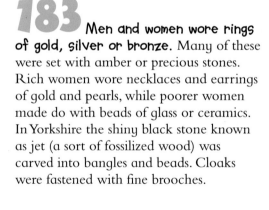

Eat, drink and be merry!

186 Roman kitchens included ovens for baking bread, raised brick hearths for boiling and simmering and spits for roasting. Oil and other foods were stored in large pottery jars. Hung up in the kitchen you might find a hare or a duck and spread out on the tables would be herbs, spices and vegetables.

▼ Food was cooked in pots and pans made of iron, bronze or pottery. Meals were prepared by slaves.

Charcoal was burned in the stove

187 The Romans did not start the day with a big breakfast, just bread and fruit, if they ate it at all. Lunch might be a light meal of leftovers from the night before. Many people in towns would buy a quick snack from a stall on the street, perhaps a hot meat pie, a sausage or a sweet pastry. The main meal, *cena* ('kay-nah'), was eaten in the evening. It might include three courses with meat or fish, vegetables and fruit.

188 A Roman banquet was a special event. The guests would eat lying on couches around a low table. A dining room with three couches was called a *triclinium*. Servants would bring in up to seven or eight courses. There would be starters, salads, dumplings, omelettes and shellfish. Main dishes might include kidneys, liver, roast venison in plum sauce or young goat cooked in cream.

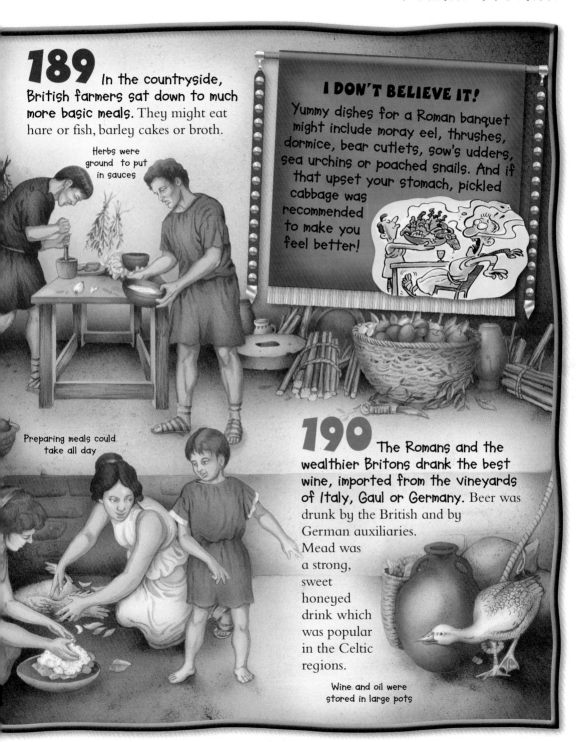

189 In the countryside, British farmers sat down to much more basic meals. They might eat hare or fish, barley cakes or broth.

Herbs were ground to put in sauces

Preparing meals could take all day

I DON'T BELIEVE IT!

Yummy dishes for a Roman banquet might include moray eel, thrushes, dormice, bear cutlets, sow's udders, sea urchins or poached snails. And if that upset your stomach, pickled cabbage was recommended to make you feel better!

190 The Romans and the wealthier Britons drank the best wine, imported from the vineyards of Italy, Gaul or Germany. Beer was drunk by the British and by German auxiliaries. Mead was a strong, sweet honeyed drink which was popular in the Celtic regions.

Wine and oil were stored in large pots

A new faith

191 By the AD 200s yet another foreign religion was attracting followers in Britannia. It was called Christianity. Christians believed that Jesus Christ, born in a part of the Roman empire called Judaea, was the son of God. They taught that he had been killed on Roman orders but had then arisen from the dead and gone to heaven.

▼ The face of Jesus is shown on this floor mosaic from Dorset. The symbol XP (behind the head) is Greek, standing for chi and rho, the first two letters of the name of Christ.

192 At first the Romans punished the Christians for believing that their God was more powerful than the emperor. Even so, the new faith spread quickly, first among the Britons and then the Romans, rich and poor alike.

◄ One Romanized Briton called Alban was executed in Verulamium in AD 209 because he had helped a Christian priest. He was later made a saint and the town was given his name, St Albans.

193 The emperor Constantine made Christianity legal and in AD 324 it became the official religion of the empire. Worship of the old gods was still practised in the countryside.

◀ Constantine, son of emperor Constantius, addressing troops in York. In AD 306 the legions serving in York proclaimed their backing for Constantine, who had been a successful soldier. He succeeded his father as emperor and became known as Constantine the Great.

194 We know that Christianity spread quickly through Britain in the 300s. There are Christian burial grounds and chapels. Silver chalices have been found, the cups from which Christian drink wine as part of their worship. Lead tanks have been discovered too, which held the water in which new Christians were baptized.

Silver plaque

Silver chalice

QUIZ
Christian bishops were appointed in these Roman towns. Can you unscramble the letters to discover their modern-day names?

1. KORY
2. NOLNOD
3. LOCLINN
4. LESILARC

Answers:
1. York 2. London
3. Lincoln 4. Carlisle

89

Last of the legions

195 In the later years of the Roman empire, there was division and rebellion in Britannia. In AD 286 the empire was divided into an eastern and a western half. In AD 287 a Roman admiral called Carausius declared himself ruler of Britain. He was murdered six years later. In AD 383 Magnus Maximus, commander of the Roman troops in Britain, marched on Rome and won the throne for five years.

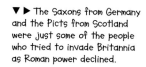

▼ ▶ The Saxons from Germany and the Picts from Scotland were just some of the people who tried to invade Britannia as Roman power declined.

Pictish warrior

◀ Britannia was attacked by invaders who sailed across the North Sea.

196 Raiders from outside the empire were circling Britannia like vultures. They wanted to test the strength of their old enemy. Saxons from Germany attacked in the east and south. The Picts were restless in the northeast of Scotland. The Gaels of Ireland (known to the Romans as Scoti) were raiding from the west.

197 In such dangerous times many villa owners buried their money and precious things in secret places, in case of attack by robbers. Some of these treasure hoards have been discovered in modern times.

Saxon settler

Saxon war chief

199

Many Britons by now considered themselves to be Romans and Christians. But they had to stand on their own. They divided the old province of Britannia into a number of small kingdoms. For hundreds of years these lost land to the invading Angles and Saxons (the ancestors of the English) and to the Gaels (the ancestors of the Highland Scots). The Britons (ancestors of the Welsh and Cornish) were finally cut off in Wales and the west.

200

Rome had ruled Britain for nearly 400 years. It had changed the history of the island for ever, with its language, its law, its towns and roads, its technology and its religion. Rome was never forgotten.

198

The Romans were in even bigger trouble on mainland Europe. Germanic warriors were crossing the river Rhine and flooding into Gaul. From AD 401 legions were pulled out of Britannia to meet the threat. In 446 the Britons appealed to Rome to save them, but no help came. In 476 Rome itself fell to a Germanic army. The mighty Roman empire had come to an end.

▶ Small Romano-British forces were formed to fight the Saxon raiders. Out of the ruins of Britannia three new lands would emerge – England, Scotland and Wales.

▶ Part of a fine hoard of Roman treasure discovered at Mildenhall, Suffolk, in the 1940s. It included silver spoons, plates, dishes and goblets.

Who were the Vikings?

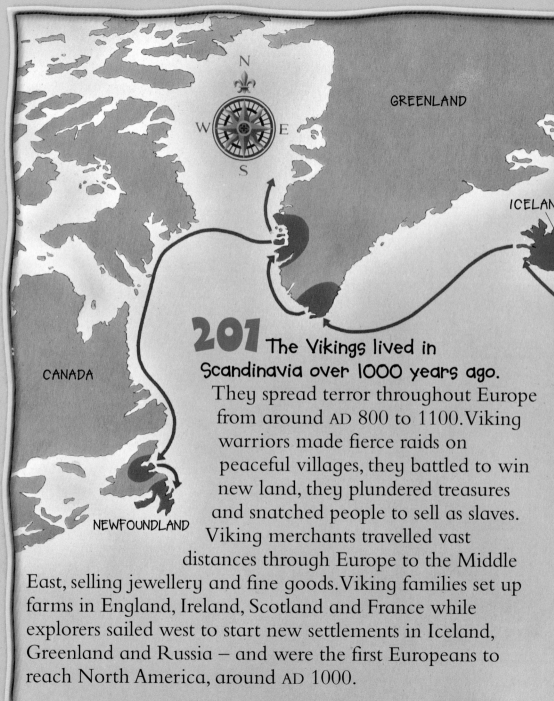

GREENLAND

ICELAND

CANADA

NEWFOUNDLAND

201 **The Vikings lived in Scandinavia over 1000 years ago.** They spread terror throughout Europe from around AD 800 to 1100. Viking warriors made fierce raids on peaceful villages, they battled to win new land, they plundered treasures and snatched people to sell as slaves. Viking merchants travelled vast distances through Europe to the Middle East, selling jewellery and fine goods. Viking families set up farms in England, Ireland, Scotland and France while explorers sailed west to start new settlements in Iceland, Greenland and Russia – and were the first Europeans to reach North America, around AD 1000.

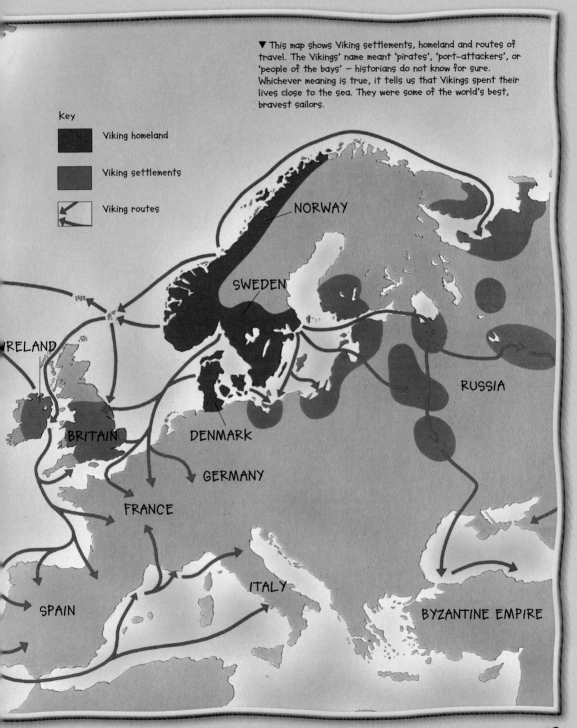

▼ This map shows Viking settlements, homeland and routes of travel. The Vikings' name meant 'pirates', 'port-attackers', or 'people of the bays' – historians do not know for sure. Whichever meaning is true, it tells us that Vikings spent their lives close to the sea. They were some of the world's best, bravest sailors.

Key

Viking homeland

Viking settlements

Viking routes

NORWAY

SWEDEN

IRELAND

RUSSIA

BRITAIN

DENMARK

GERMANY

FRANCE

ITALY

SPAIN

BYZANTINE EMPIRE

Kings and people

202 **Viking society had three classes.** At the top were nobles (kings or chiefs). They were rich, owned land and had many servants. Freemen, the middle group, included farmers, traders, and craftworkers and their wives. Slaves were the lowest group. They worked hard for nobles and freemen and could not leave their owner.

Viking slave

Viking farmer

Viking noble warrior

▲ Slaves, farmers and warriors all worked hard to make Viking lands rich and powerful.

◄ Famous for his cruelty, Erik Bloodaxe was the last Viking to rule the kingdom of Northumbria, in north-east England.

203 **Viking warlords turned into kings.** During early Viking times, local chiefs controlled large areas of land. They also had armies of freemen. Over the centuries, some became richer and more powerful than the rest by raiding and conquering lands. By AD 1050, one noble controlled each Viking country, and called himself king.

204 **King Erik Bloodaxe killed his brothers.** When a Viking king died, each of his sons had an equal right to inherit the throne. Members of Viking royal families often had to fight among themselves for the right to rule. In AD 930, King Erik of Norway killed his brothers so that he could rule alone.

205 **King Harald Bluetooth left a magnificent memorial.** King Harald ruled Denmark from around AD 935 to 985. He was one of the first Viking kings to become a Christian. He built a church at Jelling, the ancient Danish royal burial site, and had his parents' bodies dug up and re-buried inside. He also paid for a splendid pyramid-shaped, monument to be built next to the church, in memory of them. This 'Jelling Stone' was decorated with carvings in Viking and Christian designs.

▶ The Jelling stone (far right of picture) has carvings of a snake and a lion-like monster, fighting together. They symbolize the forces of good and evil.

206 **King Cnut ruled a European empire – but not the waves!** King Cnut was one of the mightiest Viking kings. By 1028 he ruled England, Denmark and Norway. However he did not want to appear too proud. So, one day, he staged a strange event on an English beach and commanded the waves to obey him! When they did not he said, 'This proves that I am weak. Only God can control the sea.'

I DON'T BELIEVE IT!

Many Viking rulers had strange or violent names, such as Svein Forkbeard, Einar Falsemouth, Magnus Barelegs, Thorfinn Skullsplitter and Sigurd the Stout.

Sailors and raiders

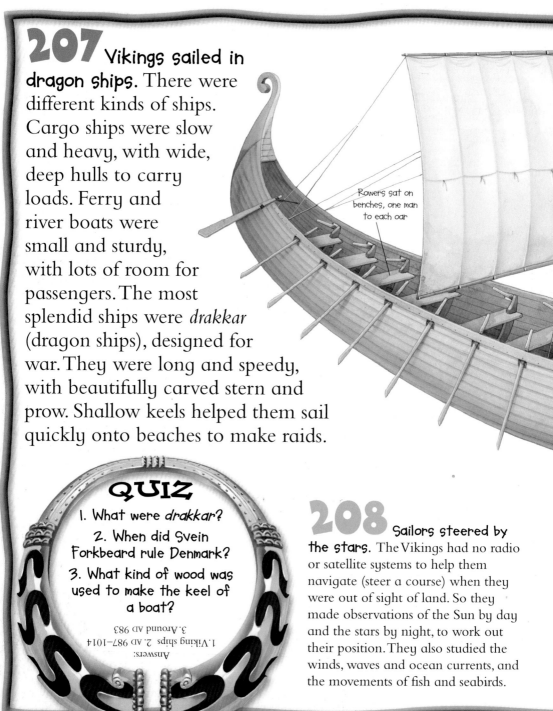

207 **Vikings sailed in dragon ships.** There were different kinds of ships. Cargo ships were slow and heavy, with wide, deep hulls to carry loads. Ferry and river boats were small and sturdy, with lots of room for passengers. The most splendid ships were *drakkar* (dragon ships), designed for war. They were long and speedy, with beautifully carved stern and prow. Shallow keels helped them sail quickly onto beaches to make raids.

Rowers sat on benches, one man to each oar

208 **Sailors steered by the stars.** The Vikings had no radio or satellite systems to help them navigate (steer a course) when they were out of sight of land. So they made observations of the Sun by day and the stars by night, to work out their position. They also studied the winds, waves and ocean currents, and the movements of fish and seabirds.

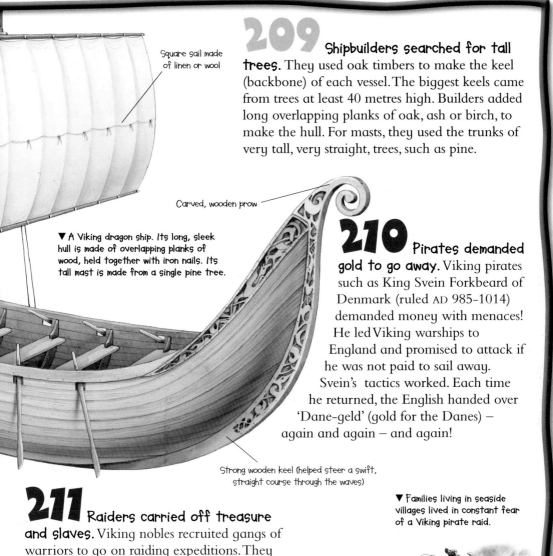

Square sail made of linen or wool

Carved, wooden prow

▼ A Viking dragon ship. Its long, sleek hull is made of overlapping planks of wood, held together with iron nails. Its tall mast is made from a single pine tree.

Strong wooden keel (helped steer a swift, straight course through the waves)

209 Shipbuilders searched for tall trees.
They used oak timbers to make the keel (backbone) of each vessel. The biggest keels came from trees at least 40 metres high. Builders added long overlapping planks of oak, ash or birch, to make the hull. For masts, they used the trunks of very tall, very straight, trees, such as pine.

210 Pirates demanded gold to go away.
Viking pirates such as King Svein Forkbeard of Denmark (ruled AD 985–1014) demanded money with menaces! He led Viking warships to England and promised to attack if he was not paid to sail away. Svein's tactics worked. Each time he returned, the English handed over 'Dane-geld' (gold for the Danes) – again and again – and again!

211 Raiders carried off treasure and slaves.
Viking nobles recruited gangs of warriors to go on raiding expeditions. They sailed away from Viking homelands to attack villages or defenceless monasteries. Their aim was to grab valuable treasure and healthy young men and women to sell as slaves.

▼ Families living in seaside villages lived in constant fear of a Viking pirate raid.

Warriors and weapons

212 **Vikings valued glory more than long life.** They believed that a dead warrior's fame lived on after him, and made sure that his name would never die. Myths and legends also told how warriors who died in battle would go to Valhalla, where they feasted with the gods.

213 **Berserkers were mad for battle.** Berserkers ('bear-shirts') were warriors who dressed in animal skins and worked themselves into a trance before battle. They charged at the enemy, howling and growling like wolves and chewing at their shields. In this state, they were wild and fearless and dangerous to anyone who got in their way. This is where the word 'beserk' comes from.

▲ Berserkir warriors rushed madly into battle, wearing animal skins over their chain mail armour.

214 Lords led followers into war.

There were no national armies in Viking times. Each king or lord led his followers into battle against a shared enemy. A lord's followers fought to win praise, plus rich rewards, such as arm rings of silver or a share of captured loot.

215 Warriors gave names to their swords.

A good sword was a Viking warrior's most treasured possession. He often asked to be buried with it and gave it a name such as 'Sharp Biter'. Viking swords were double-edged, with strong, flexible blades made by hammering layers of iron together. Their hilts (handles) were decorated with silver and gold patterns.

216 Viking soldiers lived in camps and forts.

Wars and raids took warriors far from home. Soldiers in places such as England built camps of wooden huts, surrounded by an earth bank topped by a wooden wall.

A round shield, made of wood covered with leather; a metal 'boss' (centre panel) protected the warrior's hand

Long sword

Knife

Decorated iron helmet, with a protective metal mask around the eyes

Long, sharp spear

▲ Each Viking soldier had to provide his own weapons and armour. Poor soldiers wore leather caps and tunics, and carried knives and spears. Wealthy Vikings could afford metal helmets and tunics, and fine, sharp swords.

I DON'T BELIEVE IT!

Viking women went to war but they did not fight! Instead, they nursed wounded warriors and cooked meals for hungry soldiers.

217 Viking traders rode on camels and carried their ships!

The Vikings were brave adventurers, keen to seek new land, slaves and treasures. Some traders travelled through Russia to Constantinople (now Istanbul in Turkey), and Jerusalem (in Israel). Each journey took several years. In Russia, they carried their ships over ground between rivers. In the desert near Jerusalem, they rode on camels, like local traders.

▼ Vikings made long overland journeys in winter. The frozen ground was easier to walk across — especially when carrying heavy loads.

◄ Viking merchants carried scales and weights with them on their travels.

218 Traders carried scales and silver.

Vikings traded with many different peoples. Some used coins for trading, others preferred to barter (swap). There were no banks in Viking times and traders could not be sure of having the right money for every business deal. So they bought and sold using pieces of silver, which they weighed out on delicate, portable scales.

219 Traders came home with lots of shopping!

Viking merchants purchased goods, as well as selling them. They went to Britain to buy wheat and cloth and to France for wine and pottery. They bought glass in Germany, jewellery in Russia, and spices from the Middle East.

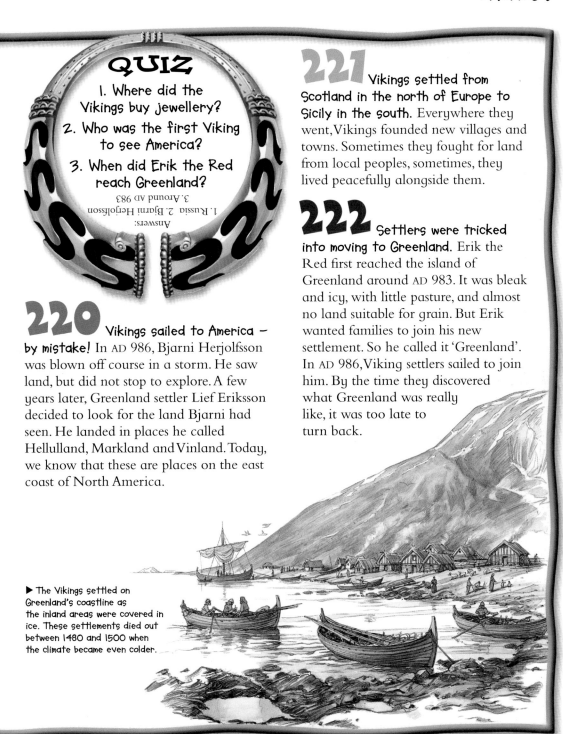

221 **Vikings settled from Scotland in the north of Europe to Sicily in the south.** Everywhere they went, Vikings founded new villages and towns. Sometimes they fought for land from local peoples, sometimes, they lived peacefully alongside them.

222 **Settlers were tricked into moving to Greenland.** Erik the Red first reached the island of Greenland around AD 983. It was bleak and icy, with little pasture, and almost no land suitable for grain. But Erik wanted families to join his new settlement. So he called it 'Greenland'. In AD 986, Viking settlers sailed to join him. By the time they discovered what Greenland was really like, it was too late to turn back.

220 **Vikings sailed to America – by mistake!** In AD 986, Bjarni Herjolfsson was blown off course in a storm. He saw land, but did not stop to explore. A few years later, Greenland settler Lief Eriksson decided to look for the land Bjarni had seen. He landed in places he called Hellulland, Markland and Vinland. Today, we know that these are places on the east coast of North America.

▶ The Vikings settled on Greenland's coastline as the inland areas were covered in ice. These settlements died out between 1480 and 1500 when the climate became even colder.

The Vikings at home

223 In the 700s and 800s, the Vikings were some of the best craftworkers in Europe. They lived in a harsh environment, with cold, long, dark winters. Buildings were needed to shelter livestock, as well as people. In towns, pigs, goats and horses were kept in sheds, but in parts of the countryside, farmers built longhouses, with rooms for the family at one end and for animals at the other.

224 Vikings built houses out of grass. In many lands where the Vikings settled, such as the Orkney Islands or Iceland, there were hardly any trees. So Viking families built homes out of slabs of turf (earth with grass growing in it), arranged on a low foundation of stone. If they could afford it, they lined the rooms with planks of wood imported from Scandinavia. Otherwise, they collected pieces of driftwood, washed up on shore.

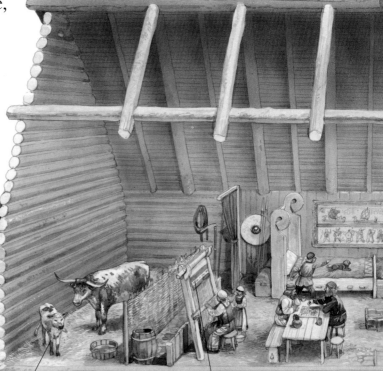

Walls made of logs

▶ Longhouses were usually built on sloping ground so that waste from the animals ran downhill, away from human living rooms.

Animals were kept in the longhouse

Loom for weaving cloth

225

Viking homes could be unhealthy. Viking houses did not have windows – they would have let in too much cold. So homes were often damp, and full of smoke from the fire burning on the hearth. As a result, Viking people suffered from chest diseases. Some may also have been killed by a poisonous gas (called carbon monoxide) that is produced when a fire uses up all the oxygen in a room.

I DON'T BELIEVE IT!

Vikings liked living in longhouses, because heat from the animals provided a kind of central heating, keeping everyone warm.

Wooden rafters

Turf (earth with growing grass) roof

Meat was smoked to preserve it

226

Homeowners sat in the high seat. Most Viking families had little furniture. Only the rich could afford beds, or tables with fixed legs. Most homes were simply furnished with trestle tables, wooden storage chests and wooden benches. The centre of one bench was marked off by two carved wooden pillars, and reserved as the 'high seat' (place of honour) for the house owner. Important guests sat facing him or her, on the bench opposite.

Outside lavatory

Farmers, fishers and hunters

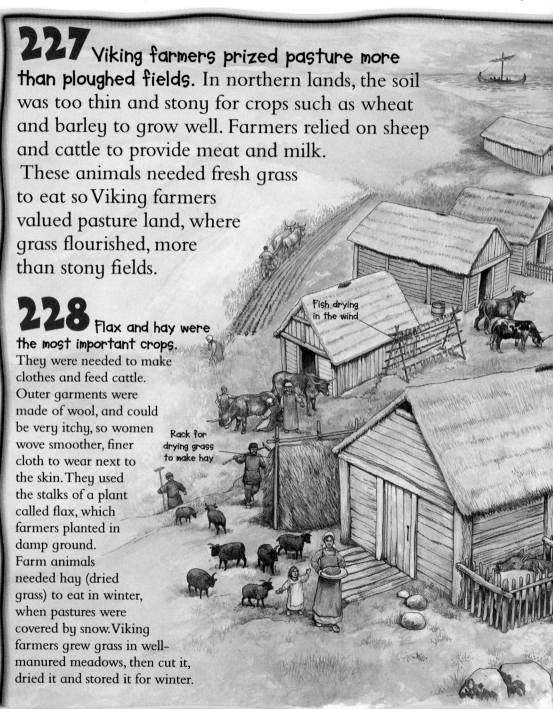

227 **Viking farmers prized pasture more than ploughed fields.** In northern lands, the soil was too thin and stony for crops such as wheat and barley to grow well. Farmers relied on sheep and cattle to provide meat and milk. These animals needed fresh grass to eat so Viking farmers valued pasture land, where grass flourished, more than stony fields.

228 **Flax and hay were the most important crops.** They were needed to make clothes and feed cattle. Outer garments were made of wool, and could be very itchy, so women wove smoother, finer cloth to wear next to the skin. They used the stalks of a plant called flax, which farmers planted in damp ground. Farm animals needed hay (dried grass) to eat in winter, when pastures were covered by snow. Viking farmers grew grass in well-manured meadows, then cut it, dried it and stored it for winter.

Fish drying in the wind

Rack for drying grass to make hay

Ships anchored in a safe harbour

229 Hunters and fishermen found food around the coast.

The Vikings lived close to some of the world's richest fishing grounds. Fishermen used nets and traps to catch sea fish such as cod and herring, or river fish such as salmon, trout and eels. They gathered mussels and oysters from the seashore, and hunted whales, mostly for their blubber. Young men climbed dangerous cliffs to collect seabirds and their eggs or scrambled over skerries – little rocky islands – to catch seals and walruses basking there.

Cutting grass to make hay

◀ The Vikings were not just interested in raiding and stealing. They realized that the British Isles provided good farmland and safe areas for settlements.

Ploughing with oxen

230 Trappers tracked wild animals.

In Norway and Sweden, there were many wild animals, such as bears, wolves and foxes. These were hunted for their furs, which made warm clothes, or were sold to rich customers. Hunters also chased deer for their meat, antlers and skins. Antlers were used to make beads and combs.

Scattering grain to feed chickens

Food and famine

231 **Vikings ate two meals a day.** First thing in the morning was the 'day meal' of barley bread or oatcakes, butter or cheese. The main meal – 'night meal' – was eaten in the early evening. It included meat or fish, plus wild berries in summer. Meals were served on wooden plates or soapstone bowls and eaten with metal knives and wood or horn spoons.

▼ Objects made from cattle horn were light but very strong – ideal for Viking traders or raiders to carry on their journeys.

Patterned silver cup used by the rich

Pottery beaker used by the poor

Drinking horn used by warriors

QUIZ

1. What did Viking warriors drink from?
2. How did the Vikings boil water?
3. What is offal?
4. How long would a feast last for?

Answers:
1. From cow horns 2. On red-hot stones 3. The heart, liver and lungs of animals 4. A week or more

232 **Warriors drunk from hollow horns.** Favourite Viking drinks were milk, whey (the liquid left over from cheese-making), ale (brewed from malted barley), and mead (honey wine). Rich people drank from glass or silver cups, but ordinary people had wooden or pottery beakers. On special occasions feasts were held, and Viking warriors drank from curved cattle horns.

233
Red-hot stones boiled water for cooking. Few Viking homes had ovens. So women and their servants boiled meat in iron cauldrons, or in water-filled pits heated by stones that were made red-hot in a fire. This was a very efficient way of cooking.

234
The Vikings loved blood sausages. Cooks made sausages by pouring fresh animal blood and offal (heart, liver and lungs) into cleaned sheep's intestines, then boiling them. Sometimes they added garlic, cumin seeds or juniper berries as flavouring. Vikings preferred these to vegetables such as cabbages, peas and beans.

▼ Viking women and slaves cooked huge meals over open fires, and served them to feasting warriors.

Cabbage

Beans

Garlic

Peas

Onion

▲ Viking vegetables included peas, beans, cabbages, onions – and garlic.

235
Feasts went on for a week or more. After winning a great victory, Vikings liked to celebrate. Kings and lords held feasts to reward their warriors, and families feasted at weddings. Guests dressed in their best clothes and hosts provided food and drink. Everyone stayed in the hall until the food ran out, or they grew tired.

Women and children

236 Viking women were independent. They made household decisions, cooked, made clothes, raised children, organized slaves and managed farms and workshops while their husbands were away.

▲ Women spun sheep's wool and wove it into warm cloth on tall, upright looms.

MAKE A VIKING PENDANT

You will need:
string or cord 40 centimetres long   modelling clay white, yellow and brown paint   paintbrush   gold or or silver paint

1. Shape some animal fangs from modelling clay, about 4 centimetres long.
2. Make a hole through the widest end of each fang. Leave to harden.
3. Paint the fangs with white, brown or yellow paint. When dry, decorate with gold and silver paint.
4. Thread string through the fangs and wear around your neck like a Viking.

237 Only widows could wed who they wanted to. If a Viking man wanted to marry, he had to ask the young woman's father for permission and pay him a bride price. If the father accepted this, the marriage went ahead, even if the woman did not agree. Widows had more freedom. They did not need anyone's permission to marry again. Viking laws also gave all women the right to ask for a divorce if their husbands treated them badly.

238 Old women won respect for wise advice. Many Viking women died young in childbirth or from infectious diseases. So older people, aged 50 or more, were a small minority in Viking society. While they were still fit, they were respected for their knowledge and experience. But if they grew sick or frail, their families saw them as a burden.

239 Viking fathers chose which children survived. Parents relied on children to care for them in old age so they wanted strong offspring. The father examined each baby after it was born. If it seemed healthy, he sprinkled it with water and named it to show it was part of his family. If the child looked sickly it was left outside to die.

◄ Feeding chickens and collecting eggs was work for Viking girls. They learned how to grow vegetables — and cook them — by helping their mothers.

240 Viking children did not go to school. Daughters helped their mothers with cooking and cleaning, fed farm animals, fetched water, gathered wood, nuts and berries and learned how to spin, weave and sew. Sons helped their fathers in the workshop or on the farm. They also learned how to ride horses and use weapons. Boys had to be ready to fight by the time they were fifteen or sixteen years old.

▲ Viking boys practised fighting with wooden swords and small, lightweight shields.

Clothes and jewellery

241 Vikings wore lots of layers to keep out the cold. Women wore a long dress of linen or wool with a woollen over-dress. Men wore wool tunics over linen undershirts and woollen trousers. Both men and women wore gloves, cloaks, socks, and leather boots or shoes. Men added fur or sheepskin caps while women wore headscarves and shawls.

▶ Viking men and women liked bright colours and patterns. They often decorated their clothes with strips of woven braid.

242 Furs, fleeces and feathers also helped Vikings keep warm. Vikings lined or trimmed their woollen cloaks with fur, or padded them, like quilts, with layers of goose-down. Some farmers used sheepskins to make cloaks that were hard-wearing, as well as very warm.

243 Brooches held Viking clothes in place. There were several different styles. Men wore big round brooches, pinned on their right shoulders, to hold their cloaks in place. Women wore pairs of brooches – one on each shoulder – to fasten the straps of their over-dresses. They might also wear another brooch at their throat, to fasten their cloak, plus a brooch with little hooks or chains, to carry their household keys.

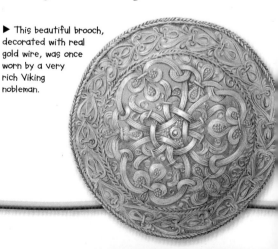

▶ This beautiful brooch, decorated with real gold wire, was once worn by a very rich Viking nobleman.

244 **Rings showed Vikings'
wealth – and bravery.** Viking men,
as well as women, liked to wear lots of
jewellery. They thought it made them
look good, but it also displayed their
wealth, and sometimes, their
achievements. Arm and neck-rings, in
particular, were often given to warriors
as rewards for fighting bravely in battle.

▼ Viking craftworkers used designs from many
different lands to create beautiful jewellery.

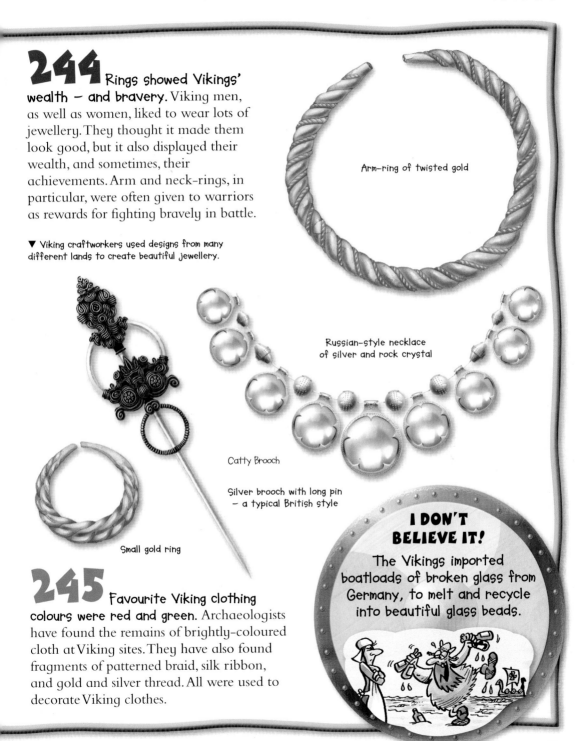

Arm-ring of twisted gold

Russian-style necklace
of silver and rock crystal

Catty Brooch

Silver brooch with long pin
– a typical British style

Small gold ring

245 **Favourite Viking clothing
colours were red and green.** Archaeologists
have found the remains of brightly-coloured
cloth at Viking sites. They have also found
fragments of patterned braid, silk ribbon,
and gold and silver thread. All were used to
decorate Viking clothes.

I DON'T BELIEVE IT!
The Vikings imported
boatloads of broken glass from
Germany, to melt and recycle
into beautiful glass beads.

Health and beauty

246 **The English complained that Vikings were too clean!** They said that the Vikings combed their hair too often, changed their clothes frequently and bathed once a week. Vikings bathed by pouring water over red-hot stones to create clouds of steam. They sat in the steam to sweat, then whipped their skin with birch twigs to help loosen the dirt. Then they jumped into a pool of cold water to rinse off.

▲ Vikings 'bathed' in clouds of steam. Similar steam baths, called saunas, are still popular in Scandinavia today.

247 **Some Vikings took their swords to the lavatory.** Most Viking homes had an outside lavatory, consisting of a bucket or a hole in the ground with a wooden seat on top. The lavatory walls were often made of wickerwork – panels of woven twigs. But Viking warriors in enemy lands made different arrangements. They went outside in groups of four, carrying swords to protect one another.

▲ Viking lavatories may have looked like this. Vikings used dried moss, grass or leaves as toilet paper.

248 Vikings used onions to diagnose illness. If a warrior was injured in the stomach during a battle, his comrades cooked a dish of porridge strongly flavoured with onion and gave it to him to eat. They waited, then sniffed the wound. If they could smell onions, they left the man to die. They knew that the injury had cut open the stomach, and the man would die of infection.

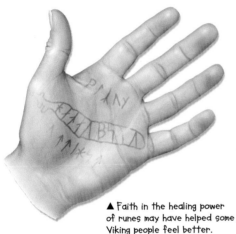

▲ Faith in the healing power of runes may have helped some Viking people feel better.

I DON'T BELIEVE IT!

Viking men wore make-up! They particularly liked eyeliner – probably made from soot, or crushed berries. They thought it made them look more handsome.

249 For painkilling power, the Vikings relied on runes. The Vikings made medicines from herbs and other plants, but they also believed that runes – their way of writing – had magic healing powers. They carved runic spells and charms on pieces of bone and left them under the heads of sleeping sick people. Runes were written on women's palms during childbirth to protect from pain.

250 Hair-care was very important. Viking women wore their hair long. They left it flowing loose until they married, then tied it in an elaborate knot at the nape of their neck. Viking men also liked fancy hairstyles. They cut their hair short at the back, but let their fringes grow very long. So that they could see where they were going, some Vikings plaited the strands that hung down either side of their face.

▲ Fashionable Viking hairstyles. Women also wove garlands of flowers to wear in their hear on special occasions.

Skilled craftworkers

251 **Vikings made most of the things they needed.** Viking families had to make – and mend – almost everything they needed – from their houses and its furniture to farm carts, children's toys and clothes. They had no machines to help them, so most of this work was done slowly and carefully by hand.

252 **Blacksmiths travelled from farm to farm.** Many Viking men had a simple smithy at home, where they could make and mend tools. For specialized work, they relied on skilled blacksmiths, who travelled the countryside, or they made a long journey to a workshop in a town.

▶ Blacksmiths heated iron over open fires until it was soft enough to hammer into shape to make tools and weapons.

253 Bones could be beautiful.

Skilled craftworkers used deer antler to make fine combs. But these were too expensive for ordinary Vikings to buy. They carved bones left over from mealtimes into combs, beads and pins, as well as name tags and weaving tablets (used to make patterned braid).

254 Craftsmen carved cups from the cliff face.

Deposits of soft soapstone were found in many Viking lands. It looked good, but it was very heavy. To save taking lumps of it to their workshops, stoneworkers carved rough shapes of cups and bowls into cliffs at soapstone quarries, then took them home to finish neatly.

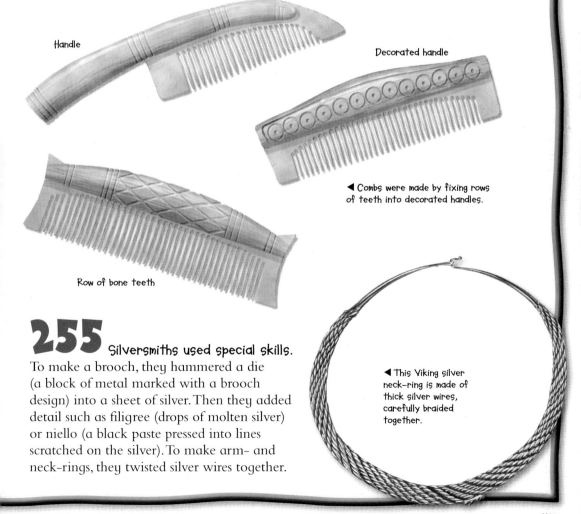

Handle

Decorated handle

◄ Combs were made by fixing rows of teeth into decorated handles.

Row of bone teeth

255 Silversmiths used special skills.

To make a brooch, they hammered a die (a block of metal marked with a brooch design) into a sheet of silver. Then they added detail such as filigree (drops of molten silver) or niello (a black paste pressed into lines scratched on the silver). To make arm- and neck-rings, they twisted silver wires together.

◄ This Viking silver neck-ring is made of thick silver wires, carefully braided together.

Viking towns

256
Kings built towns to encourage trade. Before the Vikings grew so powerful, merchants traded at fairs held just once or twice a year. Viking kings decided to build towns so that trade could continue all year round. Taxes were collected from the people and merchants who traded there.

▶ Viking markets were often held on beaches. Farming families and travelling merchants met there to buy and sell.

257
Towns were tempting targets for attack. Pirates and raiders from Russia and north Germany sailed across the Baltic Sea to snatch valuable goods from Viking towns. So kings paid for towns to be defended with banks of earth and wooden walls. They also sent troops of warriors to guard them.

258
Houses in towns were specially designed. Space was limited inside town walls so houses were built close together. They were smaller than country homes, as people needed less space to store crops or house animals. Most town houses were made of wood with thatched roofs. Many had craft workshops and showrooms inside.

I DON'T BELIEVE IT!

The first Russians were Vikings! The name 'Russia' comes from the word, 'Rus', used by people living east of the Baltic Sea to describe Viking traders who settled there.

259 Towns made the first Viking coins.

As far as we know, there were no coins in Scandinavia before the Viking age. Traders bartered (swapped) goods, or paid for them using bits of silver, weighed out on tiny, portable scales. But many foreign coins came to Viking lands from overseas trading and raiding. Around AD 825, craftsmen in the Viking town of Hedeby (now in north Germany) began to copy them. Later, other towns set up mints to make coins of their own.

260 Viking traders gave Russia its name.

Adventurous Vikings visiting the east shores of the Baltic set up towns as bases for trade. Some of the biggest were Staraja Ladoga and Novgorod, in Russia, and Kiev in the Ukraine.

◄ This Viking coin shows a merchant ship. It comes from the town of Hedeby.

Law and order

261 **Vikings followed a strict code of honour.** Men and women were proud and dignified and honour was important to them. It was a disgrace to be called a cheat or a coward, or to run away from a fight. Vikings also prized loyalty. They swore solemn promises to be faithful to lords and comrades and sealed bargains by shaking hands.

262 **Many quarrels were settled by fighting.** Quarrels between Viking families often led to feuds. If one family member was insulted or killed, all others had a duty to avenge him. Feuds could continue for months, with many people on both sides being killed, until each family was prepared to seek peace and pay compensation.

▲ Viking warriors challenged people who insulted them — or harmed their families — to a deadly duel.

263
Viking laws were not written down. Instead, they were memorized by a man known as the law-speaker. He recited them out loud every year so that everyone could hear and understand them. Because of their expert knowledge, law-speakers often became advisors to kings and lords.

264
Every year, Vikings met at the Thing. This was an open-air assembly of all free men in a district. It met to punish criminals and make new laws. The most usual punishments were heavy fines. Thing meetings were great social occasions where people from remote communities had the chance to meet and exchange news. Traders also attended, setting up stalls with goods around the edge of a field.

▼ All free men – from noble chieftains to farmers – could speak and vote at a Viking Thing.

265
Ruthlessness was respected. It was tough being a Viking. Everyone had to work hard to survive and there was no room in the community for people who were weak, lazy or troublesome. Thieves were often hanged and criminals who refused to pay compensation or fines were outlawed. This was a very harsh penalty. Without a home and family, it was hard for any individual to survive.

QUIZ
1. What were the two worst Viking punishments for crimes?
2. How did the Vikings settle family feuds?
3. Why did Vikings shake hands with each other?
4. Who recited the Viking laws?

Answers:
1. Hanging and outlaw 2. By fighting – a duel 3. To seal bargains 4. The law-speaker

Games, music and sport

▲ Vikings loved magical, mysterious tales of dragons, elves and monsters — and exciting stories about famous local heroes.

266 **Vikings liked music, dancing and clowns.** At feasts, Vikings sang songs and danced. Depending on how much the guests had drunk, the dancing might be slow or riotous. Kings and lords also paid dancers, clowns, acrobats and jugglers to entertain their guests at feasts.

267 **Vikings laughed at jokes and riddles.** The Vikings had a rough, quick-witted sense of humour. They liked playing practical jokes and listening to stories about gods and heroes who defeated enemies by trickery. Vikings also played dice and board games such as chess and 'hneftafl' (king's table). But they were not good losers. Fighting often broke out at the end of a game.

▶ This board and counters were probably used for playing the game 'hneftafl', which was rather like chess.

268

Swimming, racing and jumping were favourite summer games. In summer, the weather was warm enough for Vikings to take off most of their clothes. This made it easier for people to move freely and run and jump at greater speed. In winter, warmly-dressed Vikings liked snow-based sports such as cross-country skiing, as well as ice skating on frozen rivers and lakes.

▼ Viking archers used bows made of yew wood, strung with twisted plant fibres. Arrows were made of birch wood, with sharp tips made of iron.

269

Viking sports were good training for war. Spear-throwing, sword-fighting and archery (shooting at targets with bows and arrows) were all popular Viking sports. They were also excellent training in battle skills and helped boys and young men to develop their body strength, get used to handling weapons and improve their aim.

270

Vikings liked watching wrestling – and fights between horses. Wrestling matches were also good training for war. A warrior who lost his weapons might have to fight for his life on the battlefield. But many Vikings watched wrestlers just for fun. They enjoyed the violence. They also liked to watch fights between stallions (male horses), who attacked one another with hooves and teeth.

Gods and goddesses

271 **Vikings honoured many gods.**
The Aesir (sky gods) included Odin,
Thor and Tyr, who were gods
of war, and Loki, who was a
trickster. The Vanir (gods of
earth and water) included
Njord (god of the sea)
and Frey (the farmers'
god). He and his sister
Freyja brought
pleasure and fertility.

▼ Odin, Viking god of war, rode an
eight-legged horse. Two ravens,
called Thought and Memory, flew
by his side.

▼ Beautiful Viking goddess Freyja
rode in a chariot pulled by cats.

272 Animals – and people – were killed as
sacrifices. The Vikings believed that they could win favours
from the gods by offering them gifts. Since life was the
most valuable gift, they gave the gods living sacrifices.
Vikings also cooked meals of meat – called blood-
offerings – to share with the gods.

273 Destiny controlled the Vikings.
According to legends, three sisters (Norns) decided
what would happen in the world. They sat at the
foot of Yggdrasil, the great tree that
supported the universe, spinning 'the
thread of destiny'. They also visited
each newborn baby to decide its
future. Once made, this decision
could not be changed.

274

After death, Vikings went to Hel's kingdom. Warriors who died in battle went to Valhalla or to Freyja's peaceful home. Unmarried girls also joined Freyja, and good men went to live with gods in the sky. Most Vikings who lived ordinary lives and died of illness or old age could only look forward to a future in Niflheim. This was a gloomy place, shrouded in freezing fog, ruled by a fierce goddess called Hel.

275

Towards the end of the Viking age, many people became Christians. Missionaries from England, Germany and France visited Viking lands from around AD 725. The Vikings continued to worship their own gods for the next 300 years. Around AD 1000, Viking kings, such as Harald Bluetooth and Olaf Tryggvason decided to follow the Christian faith as it helped strengthen their power. They built churches and encouraged people to be Christians.

▶ Vikings asked fierce and furious god Tyr to help them win victories.

▼ Njord was god of the sea. He married the giantess Skadi, who watched over snowy mountains.

QUIZ

1. Who was Loki?
2. What tree supported the universe?
3. Where did warriors go when they died?

Answers:
1. A trickster god
2. Yggdrasil 3. Valhalla

Heroes, legends and sagas

276 **Vikings honoured heroes who died in battle.** They told stories, called 'sagas', about their adventures so that their name and fame never died. These stories were passed on by word of mouth for many years. After the end of the Viking Age, they were written down.

◀ Vikings loved sagas – stories that recorded past events and famous peoples' lives.

277 **Skalds sang songs and told saga stories.** Viking kings and lords employed their own personal poets, called skalds. A skald's job was to sing songs and recite poems praising his employer, and to entertain guests at feasts. Most skalds played music on harps or lyres to accompany their poems and songs.

▼ Viking legends told how the world would come to an end at the battle of Ragnarok. They also promised that a new world would be born from the ruins of the old.

278 **Vikings feared that the world might end.** There were many Viking stories foretelling Ragnarok – the Doom of the Gods. This would be a terrible time, when the forces of good clashed with the powers of evil. Viking gods would fight against giants and monsters – and lose. Then the world would come to an end.

▲ Vikings believed that Valkyries — wild warrior women — carried men who had died in battle to live with Odin in Valhalla (the hall of brave dead).

279

The Vikings believed in spirits and monsters. They were unseen powers who lived in the natural world. Some, such as elves, were kindly and helpful. They sent good harvests and beautiful children. Others, such as giants who ate humans, were wicked or cruel. Vikings often imagined monsters as looking like huge, fierce animals. They carved these monster heads on ships and stones to scare evil spirits away.

◀ A Viking silver amulet (lucky charm), shaped like Thor's hammer.

QUIZ

1. What did Vikings call the end of the world?

2. Who did skalds praise?

3. Why did farmers wear hammers round their necks?

4. What did giants eat?

Answers:
1. Ragnarok 2. Their employer 3. To bring fertility to fields and animals 4. Humans

280

Lucky charms protected warriors and farmers. They wore amulets shaped like the god Thor's magic hammer as pendants around their necks. Warriors believed that these little hammers would give them extra strength in battle. Farmers hoped they would bring fertility to their fields and animals.

Death and burial

281 Early Vikings burned their dead. At the start of the Viking age, the bodies of dead people were cremated (burned) on big wood fires. After this, their ashes were collected and buried in pottery urns. BetweeN AD 800 and 900, people in some Viking lands began to bury unburned dead bodies in the ground.

282 Dead men and women took useful items with them to the next world. The Vikings believed that dead peoples' souls survived to go on living in the next world. So the bodies of dead Viking men and women were surrounded by 'grave goods' – all kinds of things they might need. For rich warriors, this meant clothes, weapons, horses – and, sometimes, wives and slaves. Rich women were buried with clothes, jewels, furniture and equipment for spinning and weaving.

283 Viking graves have survived for hundreds of years.

Archaeologists have discovered many collections of grave contents, in remarkably good condition. Some, such as jewellery, pottery and stone carvings, are made of materials that do not rot. Some, such as clothing, have survived by chance. Others, such as ship burials, have been preserved underwater. All have provided valuable evidence about life in Viking times.

▼ These stones arranged in the shape of a ship's hull mark an ancient Viking burial ground.

284 Vikings hoped that ships might carry their souls away.

So they surrounded buried cremation urns with ship-shaped enclosures of stones. Some enclosures were very large – up to 80 metres long – and were probably also used as places of worship. Very important Viking men and women were cremated or buried in real wooden ships, along with valuable grave-goods.

◄ The dead were laid to rest in cloth-covered shelters on board real ships. Then the ships were set on fire so that their souls could 'sail away' to the next world.

285 Vikings treated dead bodies with great respect.

They washed them, dressed them and wrapped them in cloth or birch bark before burying them or cremating them. This was because the Vikings believed that dead people might come back to haunt them if they were not treated carefully.

I DON'T BELIEVE IT!

Some Viking skeletons and wooden ships that were buried in acid soils have been completely eaten away. But they have left 'shadows' in the ground, which archaeologists can use to find out more about them.

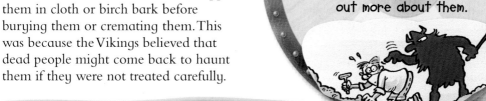

Writing and picture stories

286 Many ordinary Vikings could not read or write. They relied on the spoken word to communicate and on memory to preserve details of land, family histories and important events. At the beginning of the Viking Age, all Vikings spoke the *donsk tunga* (Danish Tongue). But after AD 1000, different dialects developed.

▲ Viking runes. From top left, these symbols stand for the sounds: F U Th A R K H N I A S T B M L R.

287 Viking scribes wrote in 'runes'. There were 16 letters, called runes, in the Viking alphabet. They were used for labelling valuable items with the owner's name, for recording accounts keeping calendars and for sending messages. Runes were written in straight lines only. This made them easier to carve on wood and stone. The Vikings did not have paper!

▼ Vikings used sharp metal points to carve runes on useful or valuable items.

Deer antler with runes carved on it

Viking calendar

Comb with runes showing owner's name

288 Runes were used to cast magic spells. Sometimes, runes were used to write messages in secret code, or even magic spells. These supposedly gave the objects they were carved on special power. Some secret Viking writings in runes still have not been deciphered today.

289 Rune stones told stories.

Wealthy families paid for expert rune masters to carve runic inscriptions on stones, praising and commemorating dead parents and children. Some boastful people also had stones carved with details of their own achievements. When the carvings were completed, the rune stones were raised up in public places where everyone could see them.

◀ Rune stones were written records of Viking citizens.

290 Picture stones told of great adventures.

In some Viking lands, people carved memorial stones with pictures, instead of runes. These show scenes from the dead person's life and details of their adventures, together with pictures of gods, giants and monsters.

▲ Some picture stones told of people's achievements, others commemorated loved ones who had died.

WRITE YOUR NAME IN RUNES

Use the chart on page 128 to try to write your name in runes. The Viking alphabet was called 'futhark', after its first six letters. It had a special letter for the sound 'th' and no letters for the sounds 'e' and 'o'. Even the Vikings found it difficult to write some names and words!

The end of the Vikings

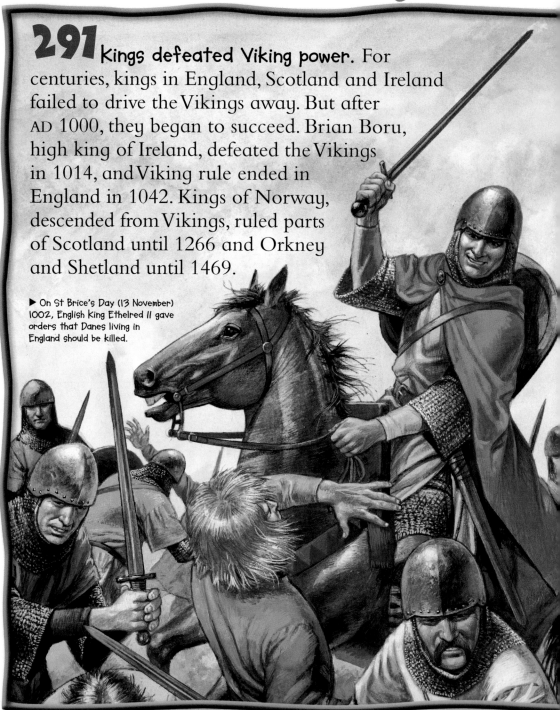

291 **Kings defeated Viking power.** For centuries, kings in England, Scotland and Ireland failed to drive the Vikings away. But after AD 1000, they began to succeed. Brian Boru, high king of Ireland, defeated the Vikings in 1014, and Viking rule ended in England in 1042. Kings of Norway, descended from Vikings, ruled parts of Scotland until 1266 and Orkney and Shetland until 1469.

▶ On St Brice's Day (13 November) 1002, English King Ethelred II gave orders that Danes living in England should be killed.

292

Vikings learned to live alongside other peoples. In most places where Vikings settled, they married local women and worked with local people. Some of their words and customs blended with local ones, but many disappeared. Viking traditions only survived if the place where they settled was uninhabited, such as Iceland, or the Orkney Islands, off the north of Scotland.

▲ In 1066, the Normans — descendants of Vikings who had settled in Normandy, France — invaded and conquered England. This scene from the huge Bayeux Tapestry (embroidered wall-hanging) shows their Viking-style ships.

293

Christianity destroyed faith in Viking gods. The Vikings believed their gods would punish them if they did not worship them, and would kill Christian missionaries. But the missionaries survived. So did Vikings who became Christians. This made other Vikings wonder if their gods had any powers, at all.

◄ Christians living in Scandinavia after the end of the Viking age made statues of Jesus Christ to stand in their churches, as symbols of their faith.

294

Vikings set up new kingdoms outside Viking lands. In places far away from the Viking homelands, such as Novgorod in Russia, or Normandy, in northern France, Viking warlords set up kingdoms that developed independently. Over they years, they lost touch with their Viking origins, and created new customs, laws and lifestyles of their own.

295

Viking settlers abandoned America. Soon after AD 1000, Thorfinn Karlsefni, a Viking merchant from Iceland, led over 100 Viking men and women to settle at Vinland — the site in North America where Lief Eriksson landed. They stayed there for two years, but left because the Native North Americans attacked them and drove them away.

Viking survivals

296 **Some days of the week still have Viking names.** The Vikings honoured different gods on different days of the week. We still use some of these gods' names in our calendars. For example, Wednesday means 'Woden's Day', Thursday means 'Thor's Day' and Friday means 'Freya's Day'. In modern Scandinavian languages, Saturday is called 'bath-day', because that was when the Vikings had their weekly bath!

297 **We still use many Viking words today.** In countries where the Vikings settled, they spoke Viking languages and gave Viking names to their surroundings. Many Viking words for everyday things still survive such as 'sister', 'knife' and 'egg'. Many places in northern Europe still have Viking names, such as 'Thorpe' (outlying farm), Firth (river estuary), Cape Wrath (Cape Turning-point) or 'Kirkwall' (Church-bay).

298 **A Viking story inspired Shakespeare's most famous play.** William Shakespeare (1564 to 1616) lived over 500 years after the Vikings. He used one of their stories to provide the plot for one of his best-known plays. It tells the story of Hamlet, a prince in Denmark, who cannot make up his mind what to do after his father is murdered.

▶ In Shakespeare's play, the tragic hero Hamlet thinks deeply about the meaning of life – and death.

299 People still celebrate Viking festivals. For example, in the Shetland Isles, where many Vikings settled, people celebrate 'Up-Helly-Aa' on the last Tuesday in January. This marks the end of Yule, the Viking mid-winter festival. They dress up as Vikings, parade through the streets, then burn a lifesize model of a Viking ship.

▶ Today, as in Viking times, the light and warmth of blazing fires at mid-winter festivals bring hope and cheerfulness at a cold, dark time.

300 Father Christmas was originally a Viking god. Yule (mid-winter) was one of the most important Viking festivals. Vikings held feasts then and exchanged presents. They also believed that Viking gods travelled across the sky, bringing good things – just like Father Christmas!

▲ This modern picture of Father Christmas shows him riding through the sky in a Viking-style sleigh, pulled by reindeer from Viking lands.

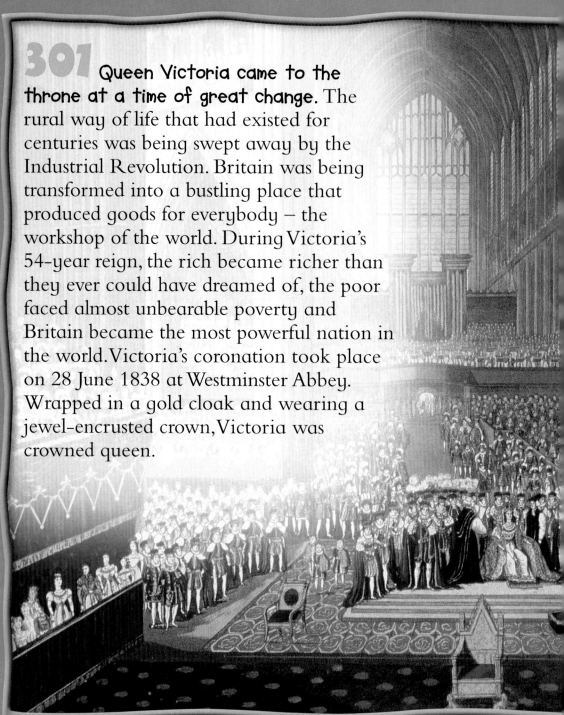

301 **Queen Victoria came to the throne at a time of great change.** The rural way of life that had existed for centuries was being swept away by the Industrial Revolution. Britain was being transformed into a bustling place that produced goods for everybody – the workshop of the world. During Victoria's 54-year reign, the rich became richer than they ever could have dreamed of, the poor faced almost unbearable poverty and Britain became the most powerful nation in the world. Victoria's coronation took place on 28 June 1838 at Westminster Abbey. Wrapped in a gold cloak and wearing a jewel-encrusted crown, Victoria was crowned queen.

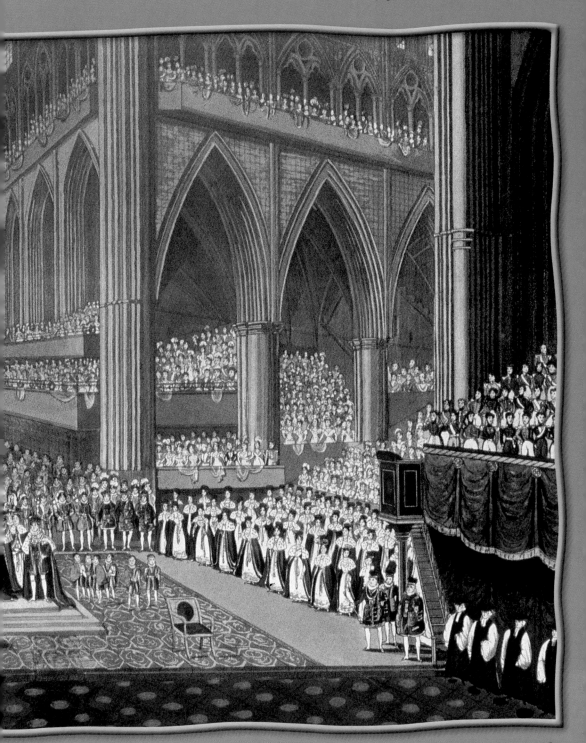

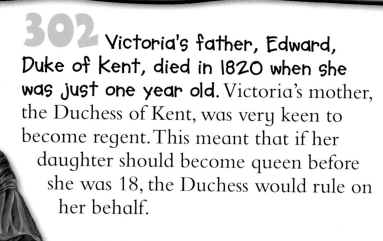

302 Victoria's father, Edward, Duke of Kent, died in 1820 when she was just one year old. Victoria's mother, the Duchess of Kent, was very keen to become regent. This meant that if her daughter should become queen before she was 18, the Duchess would rule on her behalf.

◄ The Duchess of Kent was very protective of her daughter as she was an only child. This meant Victoria's childhood was quite strict and boring.

303 Victoria was just 18 years old when she became queen following the death of her uncle, William IV. When she was born in 1819, she was fifth in line to the throne, and the chances of her becoming queen seemed very remote. But one by one, those in front of her died, leaving Victoria as the rightful successor to William.

304 Albert, Prince of Saxe-Coburg-Gotha, became the love of Victoria's life. When she became queen it was very important that Victoria married as soon as possible in order to produce heirs. Her advisors arranged for her to meet Albert, her handsome German cousin, and the couple fell deeply in love. They married in 1840 in a glittering ceremony at St James's Palace, London.

305

Victoria and Albert had a happy marriage and had nine children – five daughters and four sons. Their names were Vicky, Edward, Alice, Alfred, Helena, Louise, Arthur, Leopold and Beatrice. Some historians say that the queen was a stern mother, but others say she was warm and loving. Victoria was close to her daughter, Vicky, but had an uneasy relationship with her son, Edward.

I DON'T BELIEVE IT!

British law said that no man was allowed to propose to the queen, so Victoria had to ask for Albert's hand in marriage!

306

When Prince Albert died of typhoid at the age of 42, a Scottish gillie (servant) named John Brown became Victoria's most trusted friend. He befriended the queen during her period of mourning and even saved Victoria from an assassination attempt. Many people were suspicious of this close relationship, nicknaming the queen 'Mrs Brown'. When Victoria died, she was buried holding a photograph of her favourite servant.

▼ Like most families in the Victorian era, Victoria and Albert had many children. They valued family life and spent as much time as possible with their children. Sadly, three of Victoria's children died before she did – Alice, Leopold and Alfred.

The greatest Empire

307 **The original founder of the British Empire was Queen Elizabeth I.** She sent a series of explorers, including Sir Francis Drake, around the world to claim new lands for her kingdom. The Empire started life as a handful of colonies along the eastern coast of North America, but by the 1800s it had grown to include India, South Africa and Canada.

English spoken as a first language

English used in government

English spoken among traders

◄ With the Empire at its height, English became the main spoken language of the British Isles, North America, the Caribbean and Oceania. English also became the language of government throughout much of Asia and Africa and was widely used by traders in non English-speaking areas.

308 **During Victoria's reign, the British Empire expanded until it covered one-quarter of the world's surface.** It also included all of the world's main trading routes, making Britain an extremely rich country. Victoria was proud of the British Empire, referring to it as the 'family of nations'.

309 **India was the jewel of the British Empire.** Elizabethan explorers arrived there in the 1500s, but for hundreds of years afterwards the country was ruled not by the queen, but by the British East India Company. In 1858 control passed to the British government after an uprising, and in 1877 Victoria became Empress of India in a lavish ceremony.

310

Many poorer people were desperate to escape poverty in Britain. Some made a fresh start by moving to a different part of the empire, emigrating as far as Australia and New Zealand. Others sought their fortune in the 'New World' of America, which called itself the land of opportunity and the land of the free.

312

Not every country in the empire was happy about being ruled by Britain. British soldiers were sent to all four corners of the empire to make sure countries obeyed Queen Victoria's laws. Towards the end of Victoria's rule, there were actually more British soldiers in larger countries such as India than there were back home.

▼ The Victorians in India practiced British customs such as drinking tea. Many Indians also adopted these customs.

QUIZ

1. Who was the original founder of the British Empire?

2. When did Queen Victoria become Empress of India?

3. Which British sport became popular in India?

4. Which British custom became widely practiced in India?

Answers:
1. Queen Elizabeth I 2. 1877
3. Cricket 4. Drinking tea

311

The British exported their way of life and customs to the countries in the empire. However, local people were allowed to follow their own customs as long as they didn't conflict with British law. New British-style buildings sprang up, and some local people spoke English as their first language. The colonies had their influence on Britain, too. Colonial fashion, such as the wearing of pyjamas, made their way back to Britain during Victoria's reign.

▼ Cricket became popular in India during Victoria's reign and is the number one sport there today.

Britain versus the world

313 The Crimean War with Russia (1853 to 1856) was very damaging for Britain. Although Britain and her allies won the war, they lost many soldiers during the conflict. The poet Tennyson wrote the poem 'The Charge of the Light Brigade' to remember a disastrous part of the campaign, when thousands of British troops rushed straight into enemy fire. In total, the war cost the lives of 22,000 British soldiers.

314 The Indian Mutiny of 1857 started because of a row over rifle bullets. Indian soldiers heard that animal fat used to grease the cartridges came from cows – animals sacred to Hindus. This sparked a rebellion and thousands of soldiers were killed in riots before the revolt was eventually defeated.

◀ Despite suffering terrible early losses during the Mutiny, British troops quickly regained control of India and slaughtered thousands of rebels in revenge.

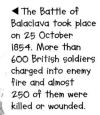

◀ The Battle of Balaclava took place on 25 October 1854. More than 600 British soldiers charged into enemy fire and almost 250 of them were killed or wounded.

I DON'T BELIEVE IT!

Florence Nightingale was a nurse who took a team of British nurses to the battlefields of the Crimea. When Florence made her rounds at night, she carried a lamp to light her way. She became known as 'the lady with the lamp'.

315 **During Victoria's reign Britain built a formidable fleet of ships to protect her Empire.** By the end of the 19th century, however, the power of the Royal Navy was being threatened by a new fleet of German ships. To prevent the Germans becoming too powerful, a new rule called the two-power standard was brought in. It stated that the Royal Navy must be twice as large as its nearest rival.

316 **In 1877, the British seized the South African state of Transvaal from European settlers called Boers.** The Boers rebelled and defeated the queen's forces, who were easy targets in their bright red uniforms. Then in 1899 British troops tried to take control of South Africa again after gold was discovered there. This time a mighty British army crushed the Boers and Transvaal and the Orange Free State became British colonies.

▼ HMS *Inflexible* was a mighty iron battleship commissioned by the Royal Navy in 1876. She had the thickest armour of any battleship of her time.

317 When Victoria came to the throne just 20 percent of the population lived in towns and cities. By the time she died, however, the number had reached 75 percent. London became the largest city in the world with a population of 6.5 million people. Overall, the number of people living in Britain had grown to 40 million.

318 Because only the rich could afford luxuries such as flushing toilets, Victorian streets stank with the smell of raw sewage. Poorer families made do with 'privvies' – closets made of earth or ash in huts in backyards. These were shared by several families.

319
The Victorian poor often scratched a living by selling their wares on street corners. People also sold fruit and vegetables on market stalls, or traded bread, milk and pies from hand carts. There were also shoe-shiners who polished people's shoes and flower-sellers who sold posies to passers-by.

320
In the countryside, the craze for mechanization meant that machines were used to plough fields and carry out other duties. While this saved time, not everyone could afford these new advances in technology. For those farms that couldn't, many workers lost their jobs.

321
In 1846 the Corn Laws were abolished by Parliament. Originally brought in to protect farmers from cheap imported food, these laws raised food prices, causing great distress among the poor. When the Laws were removed, shoppers were delighted by the falling food bills, and this also created a bigger market for farmers to sell their produce.

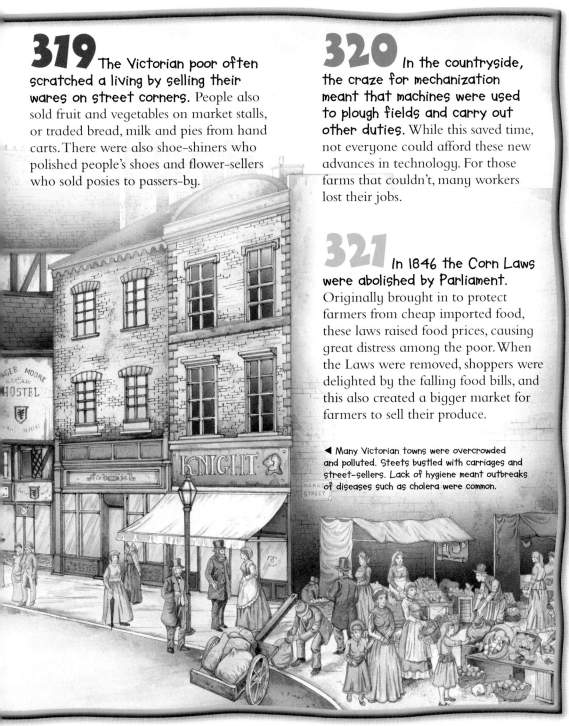

◀ Many Victorian towns were overcrowded and polluted. Steets bustled with carriages and street-sellers. Lack of hygiene meant outbreaks of diseases such as cholera were common.

Rich and poor

322 The poor lived in dirty, back-to-back terrace houses with just four rooms at best. They had no running water and one house was often home to a husband and wife and up to ten children. Brothers and sisters had to share rooms and privacy was non-existent.

▲ In Wales, Chartist protestors clashed with officials and many of the leaders of the movement were thrown into prison.

323 Homelessness was a growing problem in all the major cities. Those unable to work or too sick to enter the workhouse were thrown onto the streets. Many of the homeless were orphaned children. In 1867, Irishman Dr Thomas Barnardo opened his first children's home in London to try and solve the problem.

324 In the early years of Victoria's reign, Britain was in the grip of a depression. One group of people called the Chartists stirred up unrest by calling for the right to vote and demanding other reforms. Their fiery speeches caught the imagination of hungry audiences. Another movement, Marxism, proposed that everyone should be equal, all property should be owned by the State and that the monarchy should be abolished.

▼ Poor couples often had as many as ten children – they often went hungry.

325
The poor of Ireland suffered a disaster in the 1840s when a potato blight (disease) destroyed their crops. Millions of tonnes of potatoes were ruined and many people died from diseases such as scurvy as they had no other food source to provide them with vitamins. Thousands of people died of starvation, while others fled abroad. It took the government a long time to realize just how bad the problem was.

I DON'T BELIEVE IT!

Rich Victorian women had to suffer to look good — they wore whalebone corsets strengthened with steel that must have been agony to wear.

326
For the rich, Victorian Britain was a wonderful place to live. They went to the theatre, the opera, flocked to musicals and attended lavish charity events. This high life was enjoyed not just by lords and ladies but by a new group of people who had become wealthy through the Industrial Revolution.

327
The rich devoted a lot of time and money to looking good and living well. Ladies wore fabulous dresses and expensive jewellery (often imported from India), and carried fans from the Far East. Men wore spats to protect their shoes from mud and tucked expensive walking sticks under their arms whenever they went out.

◄ Ballroom dancing was a popular way for the rich to spend their evenings.

Get a job!

328 **Factories and mills provided employment for the Victorian poor.** Men and women would work all day on dangerous, smelly machinery making goods to sell around the world. In small clothing factories called sweatshops, poor workers were hustled into cramped, dingy rooms to work from dawn to dusk earning barely enough money to survive.

◀ By the 1850s, printing had been mechanized, which meant that books could be produced cheaply and quickly. Over 10,000 people in London were employed in the printing industry.

329 **Mining was one of the deadliest jobs in Victorian Britain.** Not only was there the constant threat of unstable shafts collapsing on workers, but pits sometimes filled up with explosive gases. To check for gas, miners often took canaries to work with them. If the birds stopped singing, it was seen as a sign that gas was present.

330
Going into service as a maid was the main career option for working-class girls. Work began at 6 a.m. and lasted until 10 p.m. Tasks ranged from stoking the fires and making the beds to serving meals and cleaning the house from top to bottom. Conditions for maids were harsh. They had no holidays, were forbidden from gossiping when on duty and often lived in freezing rooms without any form of heating, even in winter.

▶ Chimney sweep masters usually had child workers that they forced to climb up chimneys. Sometimes a fire was lit beneath the child to force them to climb higher.

331
Some people who struggled to find full-time jobs became pedlars. These poor people trundled from town to town trying to make a living from selling their wares. Their numbers included rag-gatherers, bone-pickers, cloth-sellers and animal skin traders. Some ended up in prison as they were driven to crime by desperate poverty.

◀ This woman is selling fruit. She would have worked long hours every day for very little money.

332
In poor families, everybody worked, including children. Small boys and girls as young as five were sent up sooty chimneys to sweep them clean, crawled down dark mines or wriggled under factory machines to unpick tangled threads. Many of these jobs were dangerous and thousands of children died every year at work. In 1842, the Mines Act was passed, banning children from working in mines.

JOB JUMBLE
Here are seven jobs jumbled up. Can you work out what they are?

1. diam 2. radlpe
3 michyen weeps
4. reachet 5. renmi
6. codrot 7. ghannam

Answers:
1. Maid 2. Pedlar
3. Chimney sweep 4. Teacher
5. Miner 6. Doctor
7. Hangman

Sent to the workhouse

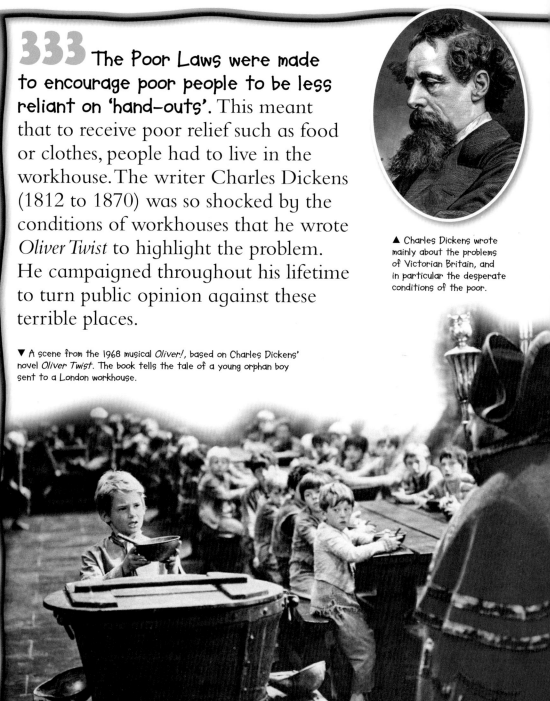

333 The Poor Laws were made to encourage poor people to be less reliant on 'hand-outs'. This meant that to receive poor relief such as food or clothes, people had to live in the workhouse. The writer Charles Dickens (1812 to 1870) was so shocked by the conditions of workhouses that he wrote *Oliver Twist* to highlight the problem. He campaigned throughout his lifetime to turn public opinion against these terrible places.

▲ Charles Dickens wrote mainly about the problems of Victorian Britain, and in particular the desperate conditions of the poor.

▼ A scene from the 1968 musical *Oliver!*, based on Charles Dickens' novel *Oliver Twist*. The book tells the tale of a young orphan boy sent to a London workhouse.

334 Victorian authorities viewed poverty as a result of laziness, drunkenness and vice, and poor people were afraid of ending up in the workhouse. Inmates were separated from their families and were fed so little that many were literally starving. In one workhouse in Andover, Hampshire, people were seen scavenging for meat on the bones they were being forced to grind to make fertilizer.

▼ Food in the workhouse consisted mainly of a watery soup called gruel, and bread and cheese.

PUNISHMENT!

The scold's bridle was a particularly nasty punishment for badly behaved workhouse inmates. What did it stop the wearer doing?
a) Moving
b) Speaking
c) Eating
d) Crying

Answer:
b) it stopped the wearer from talking

335 Children without fathers were sent to the workhouse with their mothers if the family was too poor to support them. The Victorian public were shocked by such cruelty, however, and the law was changed to allow single mothers to make fathers pay towards the upkeep of their children.

336 The treatment in workhouses was harsh, and children were often beaten for misbehaving. At the Marylebone Workhouse in London, a scandal was caused by the number of children who ended up in hospital or even dead as a result of their terrible mistreatment.

Get me a doctor

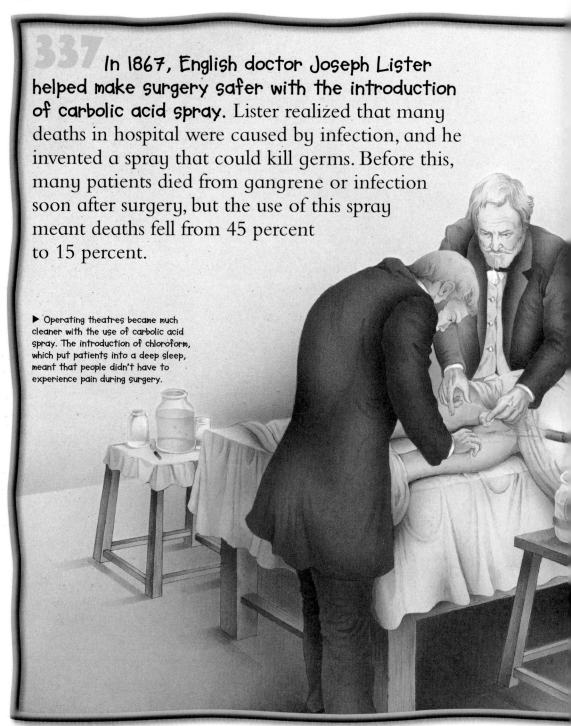

337 In 1867, English doctor Joseph Lister helped make surgery safer with the introduction of carbolic acid spray. Lister realized that many deaths in hospital were caused by infection, and he invented a spray that could kill germs. Before this, many patients died from gangrene or infection soon after surgery, but the use of this spray meant deaths fell from 45 percent to 15 percent.

▶ Operating theatres became much cleaner with the use of carbolic acid spray. The introduction of chloroform, which put patients into a deep sleep, meant that people didn't have to experience pain during surgery.

338 Around 1850, the Scottish doctor Alexander Wood (1817 to 1884), invented the hypodermic syringe. The hollow, pointed needle (which could puncture the skin painlessly) was used to inject powerful painkilling drugs such as morphine and opium.

339 Victorian doctors made surgery less painful. For hundreds of years, patients had died on the operating table from shock. In 1847 an English doctor, John Snow, started using a chemical called chloroform that made people sleep during surgery. Queen Victoria's doctor persuaded the queen to use the drug during the birth of Prince Leopold in 1853.

340 Doctors William Budd and John Snow prevented many Victorians dying from drinking dirty water. The two men realized that diseases such as cholera were carried in water, and they encouraged authorities to shut down infected pumps. The doctors' actions helped to dramatically reduce the number of deaths from water-borne diseases.

I DON'T BELIEVE IT!

The Victorian age also saw the first dentist's drill and the first porcelain false teeth!

Bright ideas

341 **During the reign of Queen Victoria, Britain was full of people with clever ideas.** Prince Albert was so impressed with the inventiveness of the Victorians that he held the Great Exhibition to show off their work. In 1851, over 14,000 men and women gathered in the newly built iron and glass Crystal Palace to show off their gadgets to millions of dazzled visitors.

342 **William Cook and Charles Wheatstone invented the Victorian Internet – the electric telegraph.** In 1837 the two Englishmen started to send messages down metal lines using electricity. In 1866, telegraph lines were laid under the Atlantic Ocean all the way to Canada using the first submarines.

▼ The Crystal Palace was a vast building, three times the length of St Paul's Cathedral and covered an area of 26 acres.

343 Joseph Swan brightened up Victorian houses in 1879 with the first working electric light bulb. By running electricity through a piece of wire called a filament inside a glass bulb, he was able to produce light. In 1883, Swan joined forces with the American Thomas Edison to create the Edison and Swan United Electric Lighting Company.

▼ Joseph Swan invented the lightbulb in 1860. The first filaments were made of paper coated in carbon.

▼ Victorians often looked stern and solemn in photographs because it took so long to expose the pictures — imagine having to pose a smile for up to one minute!

345 Vain Victorians were thrilled with the arrival of the first easy-to-use camera. In July 1857 Queen Victoria and her family posed for photographs using one of John Herschel and William Henry Fox Talbot's devices.

▶ As well as coming up with the idea of the telephone, Alexander Graham Bell also went on to invent the world's first method of recording sound, the gramophone.

344 Brilliant Scot Alexander Graham Bell came up with an invention that changed the world — the telephone. By transmitting speech electronically down wires, the telephone allowed people to talk to each other no matter where they were in the world. The first telephone call took place in 1876, when Bell rang his assistant and spoke the words, "Come here Watson, I want you." Bell's invention was so popular that by 1887 there were over 26,000 telephones in Britain.

Getting around

346 Victorian steam trains hurtled along their tracks. By 1900, 35,000 kilometres of track had been laid in Britain, while in 1863 the world's first underground station had opened in London as railways continued to develop at breakneck speed. One of the most famous routes ran from the West Country to London, and was designed by the engineer Isambard Kingdom Brunel (1806 to 1859). Passengers were so impressed that the Great Western Railway earned the nickname of 'God's Wonderful Railway'.

▲ Brunel was a great engineer who built ocean liners and bridges as well as railways.

347

In the same year that Victoria was crowned queen, the biggest ship in the world, the *Great Western*, set sail. It was a 1200-tonne monster – the biggest ship in the world. *The Great Western* sailed for the first time on 19 July 1837, and reached the USA in April 1838.

I DON'T BELIEVE IT!
Some people thought that travelling on the fastest Victorian trains would lead to instant death by suffocation!

348

Inventors were also trying to take to the air during Victoria's reign. In 1853 Sir George Cayley persuaded a servant to fly a glider across a valley in Yorkshire. Barely rising above head height, the machine flew 200 metres before crashing into nearby trees.

349

Better roads meant that more and more cars were also taking to the roads. The first practical motor vehicles appeared around 1895, and tarmac on roads meant that driving became a far more comfortable experience!

◀ The Great Western railway gave people freedom. For the first time it was possible to travel from Bristol to London and back in one day.

155

Artists and composers

350 The son of a barber, Joseph Turner (1775 to 1851) became one of Victorian Britain's most popular painters. He made his name and fortune painting stormy seascapes and beautiful landscapes. A loner devoted to his work, Turner painted over 19,000 watercolours before he died. He travelled throughout Europe to find locations with dramatic scenery. His most famous paintings include *The Fighting Temeraire* (1838) and *Rain, Steam and Speed* (1844).

▲ Turner was one of several artists who were inspired by Victorian industrial achievements — such as railways.

351 The Pre-Raphaelite Brotherhood was the most famous art movement in Victorian Britain. The group included Holman Hunt, Millais and Rossetti, who rebelled against unimaginative Victorian art. They painted in bright colours and paid great attention to detail to create paintings that looked almost like photographs. The movement received great criticism from other artists and critics, who thought it was unpleasant and ugly.

I DON'T BELIEVE IT!

As well as being a great painter, Turner was witty, too. When a woman told him she didn't like his *Snowstorm* painting, he replied that he didn't care — he didn't paint it for her.

352 Appalled by the way Britain was being flooded by ugly, mass-produced goods, the Arts and Crafts movement aimed to reintroduce beautiful handmade crafts into Victorian homes. It challenged householders to 'have nothing in your houses that you do not know to be useful, or believe to be beautiful'. The group designed wallpapers, fabrics and even houses, and their fame spread across the Atlantic to the USA.

353 Victorian music fans flocked to hear the latest works by William Gilbert and Arthur Sullivan. The pair wrote light operas including *The Mikado*, *The Pirates of Penzance* and *HMS Pinafore*. Many of these productions poked fun at Victorian beliefs. *The Mikado*, for example, mocked the Victorian craze for all things Japanese. As well as operas, Gilbert and Sullivan composed many church hymns.

▲ William Morris's wallpapers were the best-known product of the Arts and Crafts movement. The colourful designs featured plants, flowers and birds, and many are still used today.

354 Stage actors Ellen Terry and Henry Irving were like the film stars of today. In 1874, Henry Irving wowed audiences with a performance of *Hamlet*, and later produced his own plays, regularly calling on the services of his leading lady, Ellen Terry. Irving's secretary and touring manager was the Irish novelist Bram Stoker, who became even more famous in his own right as the author of the novel *Dracula*.

◀ Song-writer William Gilbert and composer Arthur S. Sullivan invented comic opera in Victorian England. Their music became extremely popular.

Telling tales

355 The most famous storyteller in Victorian Britain was Charles Dickens.
Fascinated by the poor areas of London, Dickens would pound the streets at night, making notes of what he saw. As well as Oliver Twist, Dickens wrote other classics such as *The Pickwick Papers, A Christmas Carol, David Copperfield* and *Great Expectations*.

▲ Dickens' *A Christmas Carol* tells the story of Scrooge, a miserly old man who is visited by a succession of ghosts on Christmas Eve.

356 Three sisters raised in a bleak house on the windswept Yorkshire moors went on to become some of the greatest writers in Victorian Britain.
Charlotte, Emily and Anne Brontë wrote classics such as *Wuthering Heights, Jane Eyre* and *The Tenant of Wildfell Hall.* The three sisters all died young within seven years of each other.

▶ Stevenson's *The Strange Case of Dr Jekyll and Mr Hyde* explores how things are not always quite what they seem on the surface. The novel was also adapted into various screen versions, one of which is advertised by this poster.

▶ In 1846, the Brontë sisters had a joint volume of poems published under the pen names of Currer, Ellis and Acton Bell. At the time they had to use men's names to be taken seriously as authors.

357 Robert Louis Stevenson (1772 to 1850) could write at an astonishing speed.
The Scottish novelist wrote *The Strange Case of Dr Jekyll and Mr Hyde* – a story of a doctor who turns into Mr Hyde, a nasty character, after drinking a potion. Stevenson also wrote *Treasure Island* and *Kidnapped*, all about pirate adventures.

358 Irishman Oscar Wilde was born in Dublin in 1854. In 1878 he moved to London to seek success as a writer and playwright. His most famous play was *The Importance of Being Earnest*, about the excesses of Victorian society. Wilde also wrote a novel, *The Picture of Dorian Gray*, and a collection of fairy tales.

360 Lewis Carroll (1832 to 1898) was the pen name of the Reverend Charles Lutwidge Dodgson. Although he never married, Carroll loved children, and wrote books including *Alice in Wonderland* and *Through the Looking Glass* for the daughters of friends. Carroll also wrote nonsense verse, including the poem 'Jabberwocky'.

359 In 1887, Irishman Bram Stoker (1847 to 1912) created one of the most terrifying horror stories ever written. *Dracula* is a tale about a vampire, based on east European legends, who lured victims to his castle in Transylvania to drink their blood so as to stay forever young. He had the power to turn himself into a bat, and could only be killed by driving a stake through his heart.

◀ Dracula has been made into dozens of films. This 1968 version starred Christopher Lee as Count Dracula.

▼ The Mad Hatter's tea party, where Alice takes tea with a collection of bizarre characters, is one of the most famous parts of Carroll's *Alice in Wonderland*.

ANAGRAM AGONY

Rearrange the sentences below to find the names of four famous books.

1. Wives tor lit
2. Any jeeer
3. Ada curl
4. In an odd wine cellar

Answers:
1. *Oliver Twist* 2. *Jane Eyre* 3. *Dracula* 4. *Alice in Wonderland*

Winding down

361 Thanks to the arrival of the new railways, holidays became readily available to the Victorian public. In 1841, Thomas Cook organized the first publicly advertised rail trip, carrying 570 excited passengers from Leicester to Loughborough. Cook eventually set up his own travel agency, which is still in business today. Educated young men and women travelled abroad on a 'Grand Tour' to places such as Switzerland, Paris and Italy, visiting sights such as Mount Vesuvius in Naples, Italy.

362 The Victorians loved trips to the seaside. Cheap rail travel meant that seaside resorts such as Blackpool in the north of England and Brighton on the south coast became popular holiday spots. Many people, including the royal family, enjoyed sea bathing, the wealthy often in bathing machines. These were horse-drawn huts that were wheeled into the sea, from where you could be lowered into the water by servants.

363
People in towns and cities enjoyed themselves by going to the theatre or music hall. Richer Victorians went to see the latest plays while the poor went to music halls, which were large rooms built at the side of pubs. There they could watch simple plays, or entertainers such as singers, dancers, jugglers and comics.

364
The Victorians invented many of the world's most popular sports. Games such as football had been popular since the beginning of the century, but the Victorians introduced the first proper rules. In 1863, 11 teams met to form the first professional football league. Other popular games included tennis, bowls, croquet, cricket and rugby.

◀ Rich and poor people flocked to the seaside during Queen Victoria's reign. It was thought the fresh air was good for your health.

▲ Marie Lloyd was one of the most famous entertainers in Victorian Britain, and was given the nickname 'Queen of the Music Hall'. Her witty songs were loved by audiences.

I DON'T BELIEVE IT!
Funfairs first became popular in Victorian times, with a variety of steam-powered rides.

365
Wealthier Victorians wanting to escape England's dirty cities headed for Scotland. They were inspired by Queen Victoria and Prince Albert, who fell in love with the country and bought a home there called Balmoral Castle. In Scotland hunting, shooting and fishing became popular with royalty and the rich. So did watching the Highland Games, a competition of events that included tossing the caber (tree trunk) and shot putting.

Build it!

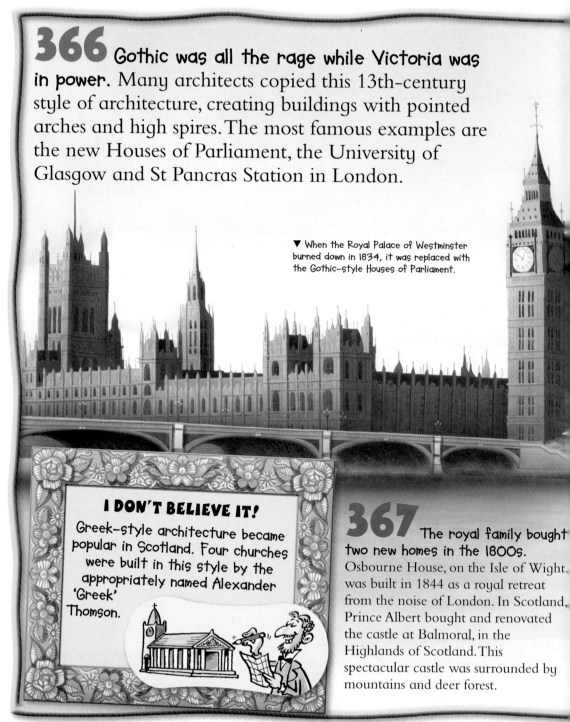

366 **Gothic was all the rage while Victoria was in power.** Many architects copied this 13th-century style of architecture, creating buildings with pointed arches and high spires. The most famous examples are the new Houses of Parliament, the University of Glasgow and St Pancras Station in London.

▼ When the Royal Palace of Westminster burned down in 1834, it was replaced with the Gothic-style Houses of Parliament.

I DON'T BELIEVE IT!

Greek-style architecture became popular in Scotland. Four churches were built in this style by the appropriately named Alexander 'Greek' Thomson.

367 **The royal family bought two new homes in the 1800s.** Osbourne House, on the Isle of Wight, was built in 1844 as a royal retreat from the noise of London. In Scotland, Prince Albert bought and renovated the castle at Balmoral, in the Highlands of Scotland. This spectacular castle was surrounded by mountains and deer forest.

368 **The Victorians loved to build with iron and glass.** Dramatic arched iron bridges strode across Britain's rivers, while at the Royal Botanic Gardens in Kew, an iron and glass frame protected the palm house from the harsh weather outside. Probably the most famous iron and glass building was the Crystal Palace, built to house the Great Exhibition in 1851. Sadly it burnt to the ground just a few years later.

369 **In Scotland, architect Charles Rennie Mackintosh was building great buildings out of stone blocks.** He designed the interior of the Willow Tea Rooms in Glasgow and filled it with mirrors and stencilled figures, created by his wife Margaret Macdonald. Mackintosh's best-known work was the Glasgow School of Art building, an imposing stone building that was begun in 1897.

▼ In 1890, the magnificent Forth Rail Bridge was opened, allowing trains to cross the Firth of Forth in Scotland. Designed by Sir John Fowler and Benjamin Parker, the bridge took seven years to complete.

What's for dinner?

370 Cooks in the 1800s had a problem keeping food fresh. Meat or fish would go off after a few days, or even sooner in hot weather. To solve this problem, Victorian inventors built the first refrigerator in 1900. Food was chilled by cold air, circulated by a pump from ice blocks stored in a special compartment. Scientists also found a way to tin food, meaning that groceries such as fruit and vegetables could be kept fresh for months.

371 Children throughout Victorian Britain were delighted by the arrival of ice-cream. A famous cook called Agnes Marshall set up her own cookery school specializing in the delicious dessert. She claims to have made the first ice-cream cornet in 1888 and published a book called *Fancy Ices* in 1894.

▼ Victorian cooks worked extremely hard. All food was prepared by hand – from bread to soup and puddings.

372 Exotic foods brought back from the farthest corners of the Empire ended up on the dining tables of the wealthy. Fruits such as pineapples and kiwi became popular with the rich, while spices such as turmeric found their way into Victorian cooking pots. Tea, for a long time a luxury, became affordable for everybody.

▶ Pineapples were brought to Britain from the Caribbean, kiwi fruit from New Zealand and turmeric and tea from India.

Pineapple

Tea

Kiwi fruit

Turmeric

373 Fresh milk was delivered straight from the farm to the doors of Victorian houses. On set days, householders would carry out jugs to the passing milkman, who filled them from large churns. The ready availability of milk added Vitamin D to the diets of many malnourished children, helping to prevent diseases such as rickets.

374 Mrs Beeton became the world's first celebrity chef. The eldest girl among 17 children, she spent most of her childhood bringing up her younger brothers and sisters. She went on to find work as a magazine editor, and had the idea of collecting recipes sent in by readers to make into a book. In 1861, Mrs Beeton published *Mrs Beeton's Book of Household Management*, packed with recipes and tips.

▶ Victorian milkmen usually carried milk in large open pails hung from a wooden yoke across their shoulders.

MAKE ICE CREAM!

You will need:
large plastic bag   ice   6 tbsp salt   1 tbsp sugar   ½ pint milk vanilla essence   bowl small plastic bag

1. Half fill the larger bag with ice, add the salt and seal it.

2. Mix the sugar with the milk and vanilla in a bowl, pour into the small bag and seal it.

3. Open the large bag, put the small bag inside and seal the large bag again.

4. Shake the bag for a few minutes. Your mixture will turn to ice cream!

Let us pray

375 Around 60 percent of Victorians regularly went to church on Sundays. New churches were built and old ones restored to cope with a religious revival. A bill to force people to attend church on Sundays was put forward in 1837, and Victorian society expected people to be hardworking and respectable.

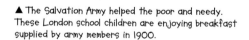
▲ The Salvation Army helped the poor and needy. These London school children are enjoying breakfast supplied by army members in 1900.

376 English religious leader William Booth founded the Christian Mission in East London in 1865, which was renamed the Salvation Army in 1878. This army did not fight with bullets and swords but with the word of God. Booth organized members like an army to fight against sin and evil. The Salvation Army's aim was to show the love of God through Christianity and concern for the poorer classes.

◄ At the age of 13 William Booth was sent to work as an apprentice in a pawnbroker's shop. This experience helped him to understand the suffering endured by the Victorian poor.

377

Many Victorians thought the Church of England was neglecting the poor. The new Evangelical Church had a more caring attitude towards the less well-off and placed emphasis on helping the needy. It had also been responsible for pressing the government to abolish slavery throughout the Empire.

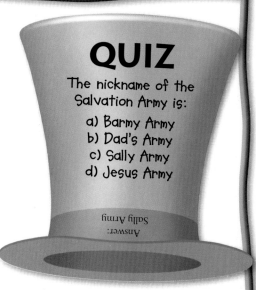

QUIZ

The nickname of the Salvation Army is:
a) Barmy Army
b) Dad's Army
c) Sally Army
d) Jesus Army

Answer:
Sally Army

▲ The remote Galapagos Islands are situated off the West coast of Ecuador. This map charts the route that Darwin took in his ship *The Beagle*.

378

In 1859, Charles Darwin published *Origin of Species*, throwing religious leaders into a fury. The book challenged the accepted idea that God created the world. In 1871, Darwin published *The Descent of Man*, which said that man evolved gradually from apes thousands of years ago. Darwin developed his ideas during a trip to the Galapagos Islands in South America, where he noticed that a single species of bird had evolved into many different kinds to adapt to different habitats.

379

Religious beliefs were also challenged by the discovery of dinosaur fossils. Finding fossils of creatures that lived millions of years before man was a shock, especially when the Bible said the world was created just a few thousand years ago. People found their religious faith being tested.

▼ The skull of the dinosaur *Heterodontosaurus*. Finding ancient fossil remains such as this made people question what was written in the Bible.

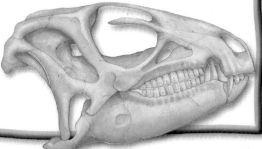

167

The long arm of the law

380
By 1856 most towns had their own police force. The first police officers wore top hats and tailcoats, and wielded wooden truncheons. They were known as 'peelers' or 'bobbies' after Sir Robert Peel, who set up London's Metropolitan police force in 1829.

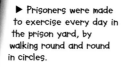
◀ Early policemen wore dark blue tailcoats with buttons up to the throat and reinforced top hats. This helped people recognize them easily.

▶ Prisoners were made to exercise every day in the prison yard, by walking round and round in circles.

381
The Victorians built lots of new prisons. Old gaols and rusting prison hulks (ships) could not cope with the crime rate, so between 1842 and 1877, 90 new lock-ups were built. Life inside was hard work and prisoners were not allowed to talk to each other. The aim was to make prisoners think about what they had done and face up to their responsibilities.

382
You could be locked up for not paying your debts in Victorian Britain. Houses of Correction such as Fleet, Clink and Marshalsea prisons in London held beggars, the homeless and those who owed money. They stayed behind bars until their debts were settled.

383 Less people were sentenced to death in Victorian Britain than in the past.

But it still remained the ultimate punishment. To make death more 'humane', trap doors were installed on the gallows, breaking the victims' necks more quickly when they dropped to their deaths.

▶ The sentence for a murderer was death by hanging.

384 Pickpockets were a plague in large Victorian towns.

Professional thieves used their quick fingers to lift items such as jewellery from wealthy victims, often followimg men and women out of pubs, as drunken people made easier victims.

▼ Gangs of child pickpockets run by violent criminals were found in all the large cities in Britain.

385 Science was helping to catch criminals for the first time.

In 1884 Sir Francis Dalton proposed the use of fingerprints to identify criminals, and soon after, detectives became able to spot the tiniest specks of blood on criminals' clothing. There were also methods for detecting the use of poisons. Less successful ways to catch villains included physiology and the studying of prisoners' bodies to try to prove that they 'looked' different from ordinary people.

I DON'T BELIEVE IT!

People were so gripped by Sir Arthur Conan Doyle's stories about the fictional detective Sherlock Holmes that some were convinced he was a real policeman!

386 The most famous villain in Victorian Britain was never caught by the police.

Jack the Ripper killed at least five women in East London in 1888. The killer also sent postcards to the police to taunt them, but he was never identified.

That'll teach them

387 In 1880, a new law stating that all children between the ages of five and ten must go to school, came into force. Because education was not free, however, few poor families could afford to send their children to school.

In 1891, the law was changed again and schooling up to the age of 11 became free for all.

388 In 1818, a Portsmouth shoemaker called John Pounds started a free school for poor children. The idea was copied by others, and by 1852 there were over 200 of these 'ragged schools' in Britain. Conditions were often very basic. When Charles Dickens visited a ragged school in the 1840s he was said to be appalled by the state of the buildings and how dirty the children were.

▼ Victorian lessons concentrated on the 'three Rs' – Reading, wRiting and aRithmetic. Children learned by repeating lines until they were word perfect.

389

Many working-class children had to work all week, and had little chance to learn. Sunday (or Charity) schools were set up to try to give these children a basic education. Children were taught how to read and write, and attended Bible study classes.

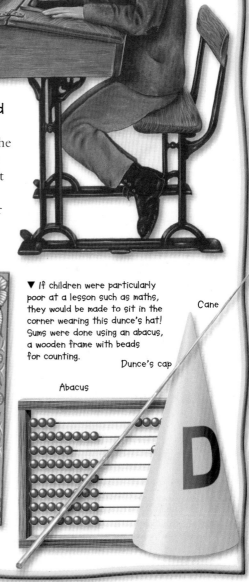

▶ School children sat in rows at wooden desks, facing the blackboard. They wrote onto a slate using slate pencils.

390

Naughty Victorian children faced punishments at school. Stern schoolmasters punished disobedient or disruptive children with the strap and the cane for 'crimes' such as leaving the playground without permission. Some teachers hit pupils so hard their canes snapped. To stop this happening, they stored their canes in jars of water to make them more supple!

I DON'T BELIEVE IT!

The most famous pickpocket is a character from *Oliver*. The Artful Dodger is a member of Fagin's gang, which gets Oliver into trouble.

▼ If children were particularly poor at a lesson such as maths, they would be made to sit in the corner wearing this dunce's hat! Sums were done using an abacus, a wooden frame with beads for counting.

Cane

Dunce's cap

Abacus

Family life

391 For the Victorian middle class the home was the heart of family life. It was a place to relax, have dinner, and somewhere to entertain friends. Working-class families preferred to spend leisure time elsewhere, as their homes were often dingy, smelly and cramped. They sometimes ate out, as cheap food was readily available from street stalls or pubs.

392 Many Victorians played games to unwind in the evenings. Battle lines were drawn over the ancient games of chess, backgammon and draughts, while darts was also popular. Children played games including blow football, Pin the Tail on the Donkey, Blind Man's Buff, Squeak Piggy Squeak and Snakes and Ladders.

▼ In the evenings, wealthy Victorian families gathered around a roaring fire to play games, listen to the piano or tell stories.

▲ Toys such as this rocking horse would have been given to children by wealthy parents to help them get used to balancing on the back of a horse!

395 **Naughty children were not tolerated by Victorian parents.** If a child did something wrong he or she would be punished. Poor children often had to go to work, but richer children enjoyed a far more pampered lifestyle. They were looked after by nannies and nursemaids, and had expensive toys to play with. Rich children saw little of their parents, however, and were allowed an hour each evening to spend time with them before going to bed.

396 **Victorians loved music.** Many children and adults were able to play instruments. Sing-a-longs were extremely popular, with the whole family crowding round a piano to join in the fun. In 1887 the invention of the gramophone by Emile Berlinger in the USA made music more readily available for everyone.

393 **The Victorians had many Christmas customs that we still enjoy today.** The idea of a white-bearded man called Father Christmas, who delivered gifts to children on Christmas Eve, was brought to Britain by Prince Albert. Victorians also introduced the practice of sending Christmas cards in 1846.

394 **The Victorian father was strict and stern.** He was obeyed by all the family and children were expected to call their father 'sir'. In rich households, fathers had a study, which the rest of the family were forbidden from entering without permission.

QUIZ

1. Which Victorian game, still played today, involved blindfolding an opponent?

2. Which Christmas tradition was introduced in 1846?

3. What was invented in 1887?

Answer:
1. Blind Man's Buff 2. Sending Christmas cards 3. The gramophone

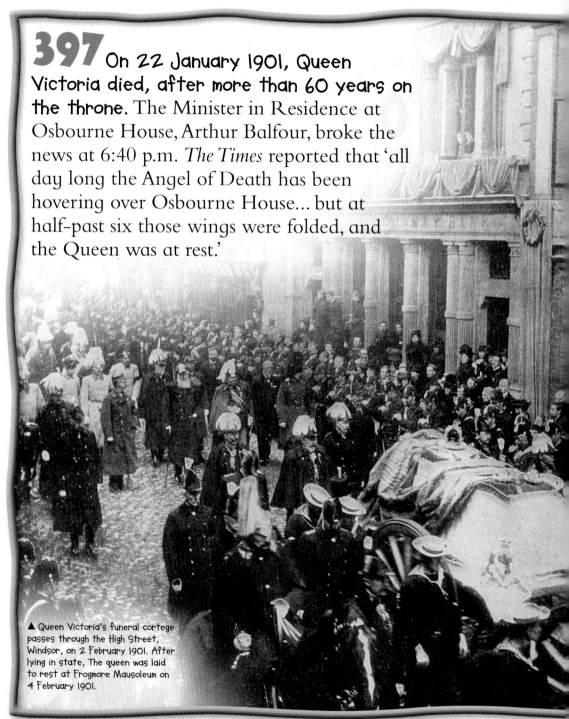

397 **On 22 January 1901, Queen Victoria died, after more than 60 years on the throne.** The Minister in Residence at Osbourne House, Arthur Balfour, broke the news at 6:40 p.m. *The Times* reported that 'all day long the Angel of Death has been hovering over Osbourne House... but at half-past six those wings were folded, and the Queen was at rest.'

▲ Queen Victoria's funeral cortege passes through the High Street, Windsor, on 2 February 1901. After lying in state, The queen was laid to rest at Frogmore Mausoleum on 4 February 1901.

398

After Victoria's death the throne passed to her son, Edward VII. Victoria had never trusted Edward, and had prevented him from interfering in important issues during her lifetime. When he became king, however, Edward devoted himself to his country, and became well-liked by the British public and across Europe.

◀ Kaiser Wilhelm II of Germany. Some people blamed the Kaiser for the start of World War I.

▲ Edward VII proved to be a good foreign ambassador for Britain as he was related to many of the European royal houses.

399

When he became king, Edward VII faced an immediate challenge from Germany. Led by Kaiser Wilhelm II, Victoria's grandson, the country began building its fleet of ships until it rivalled the Royal Navy in size. Four years after Edward died, the two countries were at war with each other.

400

King Edward VII tried to make life better for ordinary people. In 1902 he supported a new law making secondary education cheaper, and helped establish old age pensions in 1908. Despite this, the divide between rich and poor continued to grow, and it was not until the World War 1 in 1914 that people began to question their positions in society.

I DON'T BELIEVE IT!

When Victoria's death was announced, people wore black, and black and purple banners were hung from shop windows. Iron fences were given a fresh coat of black paint to mark the occasion.

Rebel against Rome

401 Queen Boudicca led a rebellion against Roman rule. Boudicca was wife of Prasutagus, king of a Celtic tribe who lived in eastern England. After his death, the Romans took over his kingdom. Boudicca was furious so, in AD 61, she led an army of Celtic tribes to attack Roman towns. After several Celtic successes, the Romans fought back and defeated the Celts. Rather than surrender, Boudicca took deadly poison and died. The Romans ruled most of Britain until AD 410 when they marched away leaving Celtic kings and queens in control. We know little about them. In fact, the most famous Celtic ruler – King Arthur – may never have existed!

▶ Queen Boudicca and her troops destroyed London. During her rebellion over 70,000 people were killed.

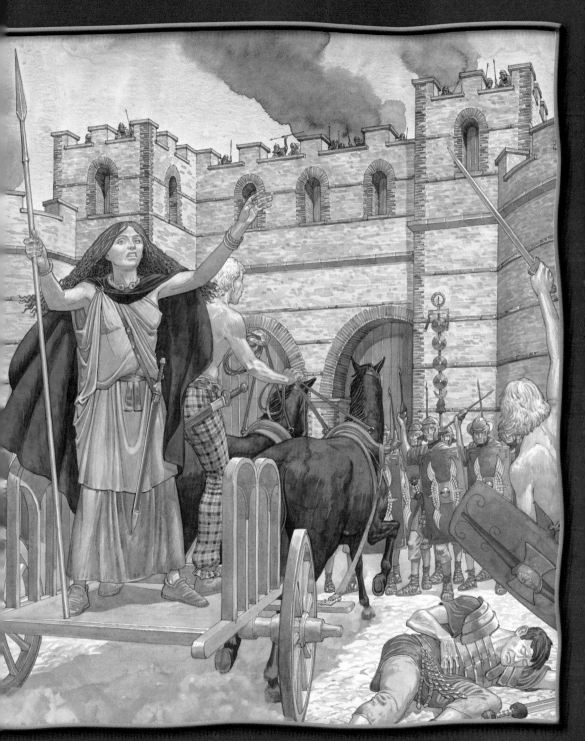

The first English kings

402 King Alfred the Great ruled the Anglo-Saxon kingdom of Wessex from AD 871 to 899. At that time, Wessex was being attacked by Viking warriors. After several years, Alfred defeated them and gave his attention to building new towns. He encouraged scholars and was the very first English king to learn to read and write.

◀ This jewelled pointer was made for King Alfred and is decorated with his portrait. It was used to help follow lines of text on a page when reading.

403 King Offa ordered that a wall be built between his kingdom and Wales, to guard the border. King Offa, who ruled from AD 757 to 796, was king of Mercia, in the midlands. He is remembered for minting the first silver penny coins and for Offa's Dyke, much of which still stands today.

▶ This penny coin, made from real silver, is decorated with King Offa's portrait and his name.

404 Athelstan was the first king to rule all England. Until Athelstan's reign, AD 924 to 939, England was split into many warring kingdoms. Athelstan took control of them all. Then he led the English to victory against the Vikings and the Scots in AD 937.

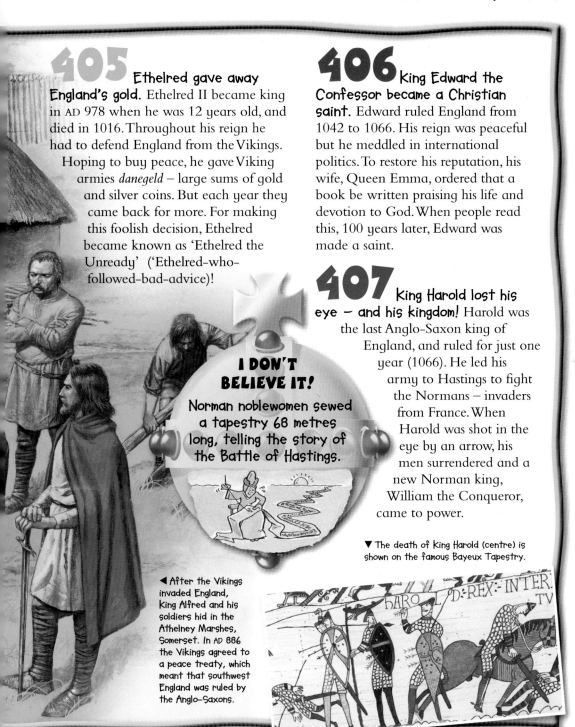

405 Ethelred gave away England's gold. Ethelred II became king in AD 978 when he was 12 years old, and died in 1016. Throughout his reign he had to defend England from the Vikings. Hoping to buy peace, he gave Viking armies *danegeld* – large sums of gold and silver coins. But each year they came back for more. For making this foolish decision, Ethelred became known as 'Ethelred the Unready' ('Ethelred-who-followed-bad-advice)!

406 King Edward the Confessor became a Christian saint. Edward ruled England from 1042 to 1066. His reign was peaceful but he meddled in international politics. To restore his reputation, his wife, Queen Emma, ordered that a book be written praising his life and devotion to God. When people read this, 100 years later, Edward was made a saint.

407 King Harold lost his eye – and his kingdom! Harold was the last Anglo-Saxon king of England, and ruled for just one year (1066). He led his army to Hastings to fight the Normans – invaders from France. When Harold was shot in the eye by an arrow, his men surrendered and a new Norman king, William the Conqueror, came to power.

I DON'T BELIEVE IT!

Norman noblewomen sewed a tapestry 68 metres long, telling the story of the Battle of Hastings.

▼ The death of King Harold (centre) is shown on the famous Bayeux Tapestry.

◄ After the Vikings invaded England, King Alfred and his soldiers hid in the Athelney Marshes, Somerset. In AD 886 the Vikings agreed to a peace treaty, which meant that southwest England was ruled by the Anglo-Saxons.

Vikings in power

408 **Cnut the Great was the most powerful Viking ruler.** He was king of Denmark, Norway and England from 1016 to 1035. Although he was a harsh ruler, Cnut claimed to be a good Christian. To prove it, he staged a strange event on an English beach. He walked down to the sea, then commanded the waves to obey him. When they did not, he said, 'This proves that I am weak. Only God can control the sea.'

◀ King Cnut claimed to be weak, but in fact he ruled a large empire. He used his power as king to bring peace, which lasted until he died.

409 **Erik Bloodaxe was a murderer – and was murdered.** When his father died, he killed both his brothers so he could become king of Norway. To escape punishment he fled to England, where he ruled the Viking kingdom of York in AD 948, and again from AD 952 to 954. But enemies there forced him to leave and murdered him as he tried to escape.

410 **Sven Forkbeard ruled England for just five weeks.** Sven was king of Denmark from AD 998 to 1014. He led many Viking raids on Britain. Then in 1013 Sven invaded England, declared himself king and forced the English royal family to flee to France. Just five weeks later he fell ill and died.

411

Sigurd the Stout had a magic flag. Between AD 985 and 1014, Sigurd ruled many Scottish islands. He had a flag with a picture of a raven on it. Sigurd believed that whoever carried this flag was sure of victory for his army – but would die himself. In 1014 Sigurd carried his flag at the Battle of Clontarf, while fighting to win more land. He died – and his army lost the battle.

412

Thorfinn the Mighty – Viking and law-maker. Thorfinn was ruler of the Orkney Islands, off the north coast of Scotland, from 1020 to 1065. Since 900, the islands had been under Viking control. But this did not stop Scottish tribes from attacking. Thorfinn defended the islands against the Scots, then spent the rest of his reign planning new ways in which to govern and making new laws.

▲ After Sigurd the Stout lost the Battle of Clontarf, Viking power in Ireland began to decline.

ROYAL QUIZ

1. What kingdom was ruled by Eric Bloodaxe?
2. Who ruled England for just five weeks?
3. What was on the flag of Sigurd the Stout?
4. Did King Cnut stop the waves?

413

Viking king Sihtric Silkbeard was a warlord who wanted peace. He ruled Dublin, in Ireland, from AD 989 to 1036, but his lands were often attacked by Irish kings. To make peace, Sihtric married one of their daughters. Later, he gave up the kingship and went on two pilgrimages to the holy city of Rome. Unfortunately, he was murdered on his return journey in 1042.

Answers:
1. The Viking kingdom of York 2. Sven Forkbeard 3. A raven 4. No

New nations

414 Niall of the Nine Hostages was a pirate chief. Niall Noigiallach ruled the Irish kingdom of Tara from AD 445 to 452. He made many pirate raids along the west coast of Britain, to seize slaves and plunder. Legends say that Niall was the first high king of Ireland, and the ancestor of the powerful O'Neill family, who ruled Ireland for hundreds of years.

415 Brian Ború fought to drive Viking invaders away. King of Munster in Ireland from AD 976 to 1014, and also Ireland's high king, Brian won many victories. The most important was at Dublin in AD 999, when Brian drove Viking settlers out of the city. But Vikings returned and befriended Brian's Irish enemies. He was killed in the fighting that followed.

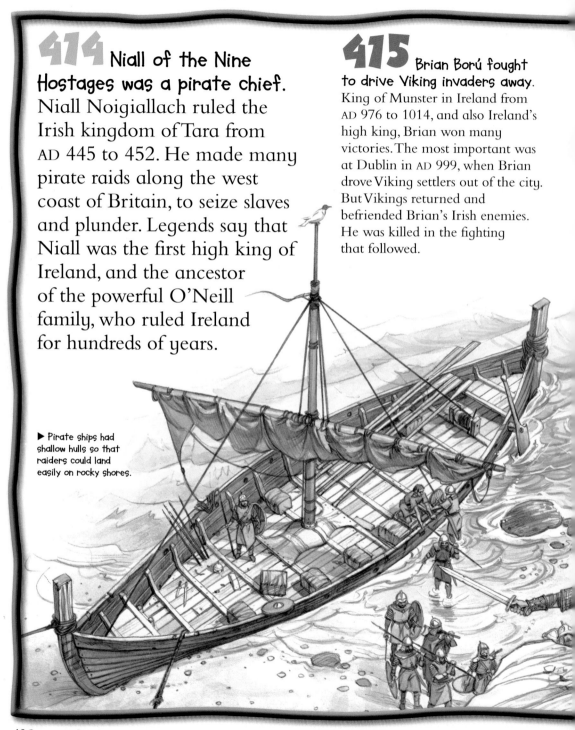

▶ Pirate ships had shallow hulls so that raiders could land easily on rocky shores.

416 Rhodri Mawr (the Great) ruled Gwynedd, in north Wales, from AD 844 to 878. He fought to defend his kingdom and win land, riches and power. Rhodri also expanded his kingdom by marrying Princess Angharad, daughter of the ruler of the Welsh kingdom of Ceredigion. He took over her father's lands and became the first king to rule almost all of Wales.

417 No one knows where Cinead (Kenneth) MacAlpine came from. But he soon became famous throughout Scotland for his brave – but bloodthirsty – fighting skills. At that time the Scots and Picts ruled two separate kingdoms in Scotland. Cinead conquered both and became the first king of Scotland, from AD 840 to 858.

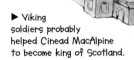

▶ Viking soldiers probably helped Cinead MacAlpine to become king of Scotland.

418 People remember Macbeth as the murderous, haunted hero of a play written by William Shakespeare. But Macbeth was a real king who ruled Scotland from 1040 to 1057. Macbeth's life was certainly violent. To win power, he burned his chief rival alive, married his widow, then fought and killed another Scottish noble who wanted to be king. Once in power, Macbeth ruled wisely, defending Scotland from invasions and protecting the Church.

183

English – keep out!

419 **Llywelyn the Great demanded loyalty.** Prince of Gwynedd (North Wales) from 1194 to 1240, Llywelyn created a government to unite Wales and introduced new ways of ruling. He also gave orders for traditional laws to be gathered and written down and collected taxes in money – rather than in cattle or corn!

▲ Llywelyn the Great fought against rival princes and forced them to swear loyalty to him and his son.

420 **Llywelyn ap Gruffudd (the Last) was prince of Wales from 1246 to 1282.** His reign began gloriously, as he led the Welsh to fight against English invaders. But it ended in disaster. English king Edward I sent soldiers to kill Llywelyn. They cut off his head and took it to London where it was crowned with ivy and put on a spiked pole. Llywelyn was the last Welsh prince to rule Wales.

◄ While planning his next battle against King Edward, Llywelyn ap Gruffudd was killed by English soldiers.

421 One king's protector turned into his ruler. From 1132 to 1166, Dairmait Mac Murchadha (Dermot Mac Murrough) was king of Leinster, in Ireland. Then his enemies chased him to England, where he sought refuge with Henry II. Dermot returned to Ireland in 1169 and Henry sent soldiers to protect his kingdom. At first Dermot welcomed them, but they soon took over his lands. For the next 800 years, and more, English kings claimed the right to rule Ireland.

▶ Robert Bruce became one of Scotland's national heroes, along with other fighters for independence, such as 'Braveheart' William Wallace (executed 1305).

422 Scottish nobleman Robert Bruce lived at a time when English kings were trying to conquer Scotland and Wales. The Scots crowned Bruce king in 1306. At first his armies were defeated, but he would not give in. A story tells how, while hiding in a cave, Bruce watched a spider making efforts to repair its web. This inspired him to go on fighting, and the English finally recognized Scotland's independence in 1328.

I DON'T BELIEVE IT!

James I of Scotland was murdered in a sewer. He was escaping enemies through a drainpipe but became stuck because he was too fat!

Kings of Scotland

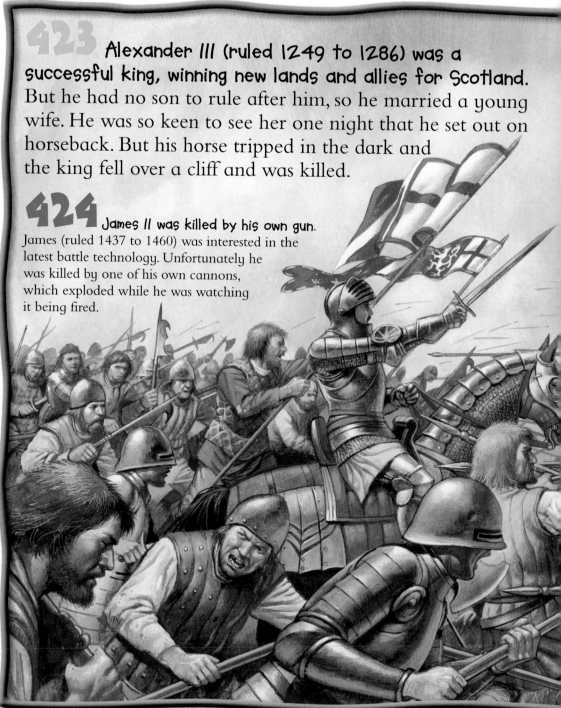

423   Alexander III (ruled 1249 to 1286) was a successful king, winning new lands and allies for Scotland. But he had no son to rule after him, so he married a young wife. He was so keen to see her one night that he set out on horseback. But his horse tripped in the dark and the king fell over a cliff and was killed.

424   James II was killed by his own gun. James (ruled 1437 to 1460) was interested in the latest battle technology. Unfortunately he was killed by one of his own cannons, which exploded while he was watching it being fired.

425

The tough ruler of Scotland from 1460 to 1488, James III made many enemies. One lord kidnapped him, another locked him in prison, and his own son helped plan the plot that finally killed him. James was stabbed to death as he slept in a cottage, where he was sheltering after a battle.

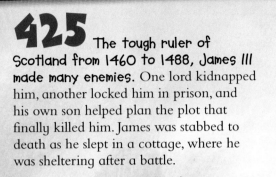

▼ James IV and leading Scottish nobles were killed by the English army at the Battle of Flodden in 1513.

426

James IV was a soldier, scholar and sportsman. He ruled from 1488 to 1513 and won fame as a fighter. He was also intelligent, sensible and fond of sport (especially jousting). James built palaces, helped schools and universities, and licensed Scotland's first printing press. He died at the Battle of Flodden, a defeat that marked the end of Scotland's power as an independent country.

James IV

MAKE SOME FLAGS

Try making these English and Scottish flags

You will need:

scissors   old sheet   pencil
fabric paint   bamboo canes
sticky tape

1. Cut out a rectangle of cloth from the sheet.

2. In pencil mark out your chosen design.

3. Use fabric paint to colour the flags, like the designs below.

4. Attach the flags to the bamboo cane with sticky tape.

Scotland

England

Norman conquerors

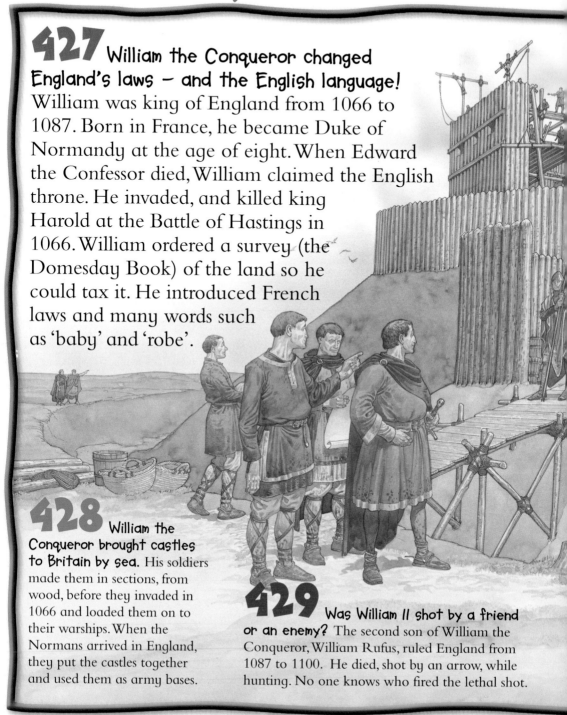

427 **William the Conqueror changed England's laws – and the English language!** William was king of England from 1066 to 1087. Born in France, he became Duke of Normandy at the age of eight. When Edward the Confessor died, William claimed the English throne. He invaded, and killed king Harold at the Battle of Hastings in 1066. William ordered a survey (the Domesday Book) of the land so he could tax it. He introduced French laws and many words such as 'baby' and 'robe'.

428 **William the Conqueror brought castles to Britain by sea.** His soldiers made them in sections, from wood, before they invaded in 1066 and loaded them on to their warships. When the Normans arrived in England, they put the castles together and used them as army bases.

429 **Was William II shot by a friend or an enemy?** The second son of William the Conqueror, William Rufus, ruled England from 1087 to 1100. He died, shot by an arrow, while hunting. No one knows who fired the lethal shot.

430

Henry I, the third son of William the Conqueror, was well educated. He is only the second English king whom we know for certain could read and write. He became king in 1100 but had to fight his brothers to keep power. Henry won, and ruled for 35 years.

431

Henry I left no son to rule after him. When Henry died in 1135, Stephen, his nephew, claimed the right to be king. But Henry's daughter, Matilda, was furious. Henry had promised that she would be queen. In 1141 Matilda raised an army to fight Stephen. Although Stephen won he was forced to agree to Matilda's eldest son becoming king after him.

▲ The Normans built simple 'motte and bailey' castles. Each had a wooden tower, standing on a tall earth mound called a 'motte', in Norman French, surrounded by a strong wooden fence called a 'bailey'.

I DON'T BELIEVE IT!
Henry I died from eating too many eels!

432

Empress Matilda was the daughter of Henry I — and she was as fierce as her father. Matilda was brave, too. After she was captured in the war against Stephen, she escaped from Oxford Castle through thick snowdrifts, disguised in a white cloak.

Quarrelsome kings

433 **Henry II was strong and determined.**
Between 1154 and 1189 he passed many strict new laws. But he could not make his wife, the French princess Eleanor of Aquitaine, obey him. In 1173 she led a rebellion against him because of the way he was ruling her family's lands in France. Henry imprisoned her for life.

434 **For years, Henry II relied on his friend, Thomas Becket, to help him rule.** In 1162 Henry made Becket the Archbishop of Canterbury. He hoped that Becket would help him in his quarrels with Church leaders in Rome. But Becket took the Church's side. In a temper, Henryshouted out, 'Who will rid me of this troublesome priest?' Knights rushed to Canterbury and killed Becket as he prayed.

435 **Richard the Lionheart was a famous warrior.** He ruled from 1189 to 1199. Richard was a brave fighter, winning battles in the Crusades (wars against Muslims in the Middle East), and France. But like a lion he could also be savage. After capturing the French town of Acre, he ordered that all of its citizens be killed.

I DON'T BELIEVE IT!

When crossing the Wash in East Anglia, King John I carelessly lost the crown jewels in the mud.

▲ Richard I was as brave as a lion – and his enemies said he ate his prisoners!

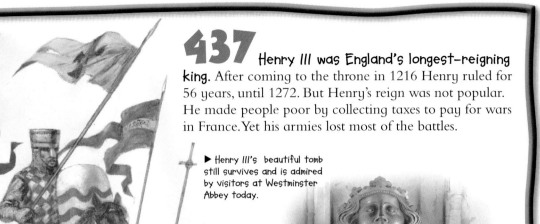

437 **Henry III was England's longest-reigning king.** After coming to the throne in 1216 Henry ruled for 56 years, until 1272. But Henry's reign was not popular. He made people poor by collecting taxes to pay for wars in France. Yet his armies lost most of the battles.

▶ Henry III's beautiful tomb still survives and is admired by visitors at Westminster Abbey today.

438 **Henry III was devoted to his family – and to his pets.** He owned Britain's first zoo. Henry spent the last years of his reign planning a new cathedral (Westminster Abbey in London), where he was buried in a beautiful tomb.

436 **King John I was an unpopular ruler.** During his reign (1199 to 1216) he faced many problems. In 1215, nobles angry with his rule forced him to issue Magna Carta. This document guaranteed people basic legal rights. But John refused to follow it and his reign ended in civil war.

▼ Nobles forced King John to sign Magna Carta. It stated that even kings had to obey the law.

439 **Edward I tried to make his kingdom bigger and better.** King of England from 1272 to 1307, Edward made many new laws. He also wanted to win new lands. By 1284 he had conquered Wales and built splendid castles there to control it. He never managed to conquer Scotland although he fought many battles against Scottish soldiers.

I DON'T BELIEVE IT!

When Edward I was stabbed with a poisoned dagger, people say his wife saved him by sucking out the poison.

440 **Edward I was England's tallest – and angriest – king!** 'Longshanks' (long-legs) Edward measured over two metres tall, and was one of the tallest men in Britain. He was also one of the most hot-tempered. He once tore out his son's hair in a fury, and broke his daughter's coronet. In 1290 he quarrelled with Jewish businessmen over money and religion and forced Jewish people to leave Britain.

▼ Edward I's Welsh castles were designed with strong 'curtain' walls and tall look-out towers. Many were also surrounded by deep moats filled with water.

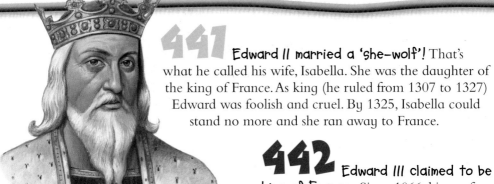

441 **Edward II married a 'she-wolf'!** That's what he called his wife, Isabella. She was the daughter of the king of France. As king (he ruled from 1307 to 1327) Edward was foolish and cruel. By 1325, Isabella could stand no more and she ran away to France.

▲ Edward III's armies won victories against France at Crécy (1346) and Poitiers (1356). They were led by his eldest son, who was nicknamed the 'Black Prince'.

442 **Edward III claimed to be king of France.** Since 1066, kings of England had owned lands in France. Edward III (king of England and Wales from 1327 to 1377) also claimed he was the rightful French king. This led to the Hundred Years War between England and France.

443 **Edward III lived in terrible times.** In 1348 a disease called the Black Death, or the plague, reached England. Victims developed a cough, high fever and black boils. Almost half the people in England died. At the time, no one knew what caused the Black Death. Today, we know that it was spread by rat fleas.

▼ Young Richard won praise for his bravery, but as he grew older he became proud and very unpopular.

444 **Richard II was a teenage king.** He ruled from 1377 to 1399. At the age of 14 he faced attack from mobs of workers. They had marched on London to protest about taxes, low wages and unfair laws. Bravely, Richard talked to the protesters and promised to help them – then his guards seized their leaders and killed them!

The Henrys

445 Henry IV was not the lawful heir to the throne. After a career as a soldier, Henry was hungry for power. In 1399 his soldiers placed Richard II in prison, where he died and Henry became king. He killed many others who questioned his right to the throne. Then he developed a skin disease, which killed him in 1413. People said it was punishment from God for his misdeeds.

446 Henry V could not wait to be king. Henry ruled from 1413 to 1422. People said he was so eager to be king that he took the crown from his dying father's head and tried it on! But the king of France made fun of Henry. He sent him a present of tennis balls! This was his way of saying that Henry should stay at home and play, rather than try to be king.

447 Henry V won a famous victory in the Hundred Years War. In 1415 his army defeated the French knights at the Battle of Agincourt. Crowds welcomed Henry home as he rode through the streets of London, which were decorated with huge figures of heroes and giants.

◀ Henry V died aged 35 from a stomach illness caught in an army camp.

194

448 Henry VI became king in 1421, aged just nine months old. As he grew up he was peaceful and religious but suffered from a mental illness. Without a strong king, rival nobles tried to seize power. During the fighting Henry's only son was killed and Henry was put in prison, where he died in 1471.

449 The battles fought between rival nobles during Henry VI's reign were known as the 'Wars of the Roses'. The nobles owed loyalty to two families – the Lancasters and the Yorks – who were enemies. Each family used a rose as a badge to identify its soldiers – the Lancaster rose was red and the York rose was white.

▼ French knights were massacred by Henry V's longbowmen as they charged downhill at the Battle of Agincourt.

Killers and kidnappers

450 **Edward IV was a brave fighter, a clever army commander and a good politician.** He became king in 1461. Edward liked food, drink and pretty women. He was also ruthless in his search for power and he gave orders for Henry VI to be murdered. When he suspected his brother of plotting against him, he ordered him to be drowned. Edward died in 1483.

▶ Edward IV won his first battle in 1416 when he was 18. Nobles fighting with him against Henry VI agreed he should be the next king.

451 **Edward IV's wife was no lady!** Few people dared disobey Edward – except Elizabeth Woodville. Edward wanted her to be his girlfriend but she refused. She insisted that he marry her, and to the royal family's horror, he agreed. Her family wanted to share in the king's riches.

▲ Elizabeth Woodville, Edward IV's queen, had five brothers and seven sisters – all greedy for wealth and power.

452 Prince Edward was 13 when his father, Edward IV, died in 1483. A few weeks later, Edward was kidnapped by his uncle, Richard of York, and locked in the Tower of London with his brother. The two 'Princes in the Tower' were never seen in public again and their uncle became king as Richard III. People thought that Richard had murdered them. In 1674 the skeletons of two boys were found buried in the Tower. Possibly, they were the remains of the princes.

453 Richard III was the last English king to die in battle. Richard became king in 1483. Just two years after seizing power, he was killed at the Battle of Bosworth Field. He insisted on wearing his crown with his armour. This made him an easy target for enemy soldiers.

MAKE A ROYAL CROWN

You will need:
tape measure   pencil   gold or silver card   ruler   scissors   glue   paintbrush   scraps of coloured paper

1. Use the tape measure to calculate the distance around your head.
2. Draw a crown shape in pencil on the back of the card. Make the distance A to B slightly more than the distance around your head. Make the distance B to C 10 centimetres.
3. Cut out the crown. Glue both ends together to make a circle. Leave to dry.
4. Decorate your crown with jewels cut from scraps of coloured paper.

The distance B to C (10 centimetres) is the height of the crown

The distance A to B is the distance measured around your head

454 Richard III is a hero to some people today. They believe that he was a good king and that the bad stories about him were invented by a historian, Sir Thomas More. He worked for the Tudors, who ruled after Richard.

◀ Richard III died at the Battle of Bosworth Field after ruling for just two years.

The Tudors

Henry VII

455 **Henry VII founded a new ruling family.** Henry Tudor was the son of a Welsh lord and an English noblewoman. He had a weak claim to be king but he won power by killing Richard III in battle in 1485. He brought peace to England, and an end to the Wars of the Roses. When he died in 1509, England was richer and calmer than it had been for hundreds of years.

1. Catherine of Aragon married Henry in 1509

2. Anne Boleyn married Henry in 1533 – she was beheaded in 1536

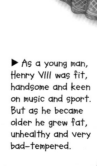

456 **Henry VIII had six wives, but not at the same time!** Henry ruled from 1509 to 1547 and lived happily with his first wife, Catherine of Aragon, for almost 20 years. But they didn't have a son and Henry was desperate for an heir. So he divorced Catherine in 1533 and married again – and again and again! Of the six wives Henry married, only one, Jane Seymour, gave him a son.

▶ As a young man, Henry VIII was fit, handsome and keen on music and sport. But as he became older he grew fat, unhealthy and very bad-tempered.

457 Henry VIII led a religious revolution. He defended the Catholic Church against complaints from Protestant reformers. Then he found himself quarrelling with the Catholic Church because it would not give him a divorce from his first wife. To get his divorce, Henry set up a break-away Church with himself as the head. It became known as the Church of England. Henry also shut down communities of monks and nuns who remained loyal to the Catholic Church – and took their money and lands for himself.

REMEMBERING RHYME

This rhyme helps you to remember the fate of Henry VIII's six wives:

divorced, beheaded, died, divorced, beheaded, survived

3. Jane Seymour married Henry in 1536 and died in 1537

4. Anne of Cleves married Henry in 1540 and was divorced just six months later

5. Catherine Howard married Henry in 1540 – and was beheaded a year later

6. Catherine Parr married Henry in 1543 – and survived her husband by one year

458 Henry VIII set up the first modern navy. He was the first king to realize that England, an island, needed a proper navy. So he paid for 20 new ships, all specially designed for war, and for full-time captains to command them. The most famous was the splendid *Mary Rose*, which sank as she left harbour in 1545.

▼ The *Mary Rose* sank after water poured though the gun-ports (holes for firing cannon) that had been cut into her hull.

Tudor tragedies

459 Edward VI never had a chance to rule.

He became king in 1547 at the age of nine when his father, Henry VIII, died. But his uncles ran the country for him and did not want to hand over power. Then Edward fell ill and died in 1553 aged just 16.

◄ Edward VI was a serious, clever boy who liked studying.

460 Lady Jane Grey was queen for just nine days.

When Edward VI died in 1553, Jane's father-in-law, the Duke of Northumberland, wanted to run the country. So he tried to make Jane queen. But Mary Tudor had a better claim to the throne. Her supporters marched to London, imprisoned Jane and executed the Duke. Jane was executed a few months later.

▲ Lady Jane Grey was beheaded to stop powerful people trying to make her queen for a second time.

461 Mary I was the first woman to rule England on her own.

She was Henry VIII's eldest child but the law said her younger brother Edward should rule before her – because he was a boy. After Edward died – and after Lady Jane was put in prison – Mary ruled England from 1553 to 1558. Mary was popular, but her husband, King Philip II of Spain, was not. Mary died without having children.

Philip II

Mary I

▼ Many Tudor people believed that religion was worth dying for. Some people faced death rather than change their beliefs.

462 Mary I killed hundreds of people — because she thought it was the right thing to do. Mary was a devout Catholic. She thought that Protestant religious ideas were wicked and wrong and believed it was her duty to make England Catholic again. So she threatened to execute all Protestants who would not give up their beliefs — by burning them alive.

I DON'T BELIEVE IT!

Almost 300 people died for their faith during Mary Tudor's reign and she became known as Bloody Mary.

463 **Soon after she came to power in 1558, Elizabeth I decided not to marry.** This was partly because of her own experience – her mother had been executed by order of her father, Henry VIII. But it was also for political reasons. She did not want to share her power with any English nobleman or foreign prince. When Elizabeth died in 1603, the Tudor line came to an end.

464 **Elizabeth claimed to have 'the heart and stomach of a king'.** When England was attacked by the Spanish Armada (battle fleet) in 1588, Elizabeth rode on a white horse to meet troops waiting to fight the invaders. She made a rousing speech and said that she was not as strong as a king, but she was just as brave and determined.

465 **Elizabeth had her own personal pirate.** He was Sir Francis Drake, a brilliant sailor who was the first Englishman to sail around the world. But he also made many pirate attacks, especially on ships carrying treasure back to Spain. Elizabeth pretended not to know about them but secretly encouraged Drake – then demanded a share of his pirate loot when he returned home!

I DON'T BELIEVE IT!

Elizabeth I sent priests to prison for wearing the wrong clothes!

▲ Elizabeth knighted Drake in 1581 on board the *Golden Hind*.

466 Mary Queen of Scots became queen in 1542, at just six days old. She grew up in France and married the French king. When he died in 1561 she returned to Scotland. Mary was an unsuccessful queen – the Scots hated her – and a disastrous wife. She plotted to kill her second husband, Englishman Henry Darnley – then ran off with the man who murdered him! The Scots turned Mary off the throne in 1567 and her son, James VI, became king.

467 Mary Queen of Scots ran away to England and asked her cousin, Elizabeth I, to shelter her. Elizabeth did not trust Mary and put her in prison for almost 20 years. Even there, Mary did not stop plotting against Elizabeth. She made plans with Catholics in England and Europe who wanted her to be queen. Finally Elizabeth could stand no more and she had Mary executed in 1587.

▶ A Catholic plot was uncovered and Mary was accused of being involved. She was beheaded at Fotheringay Castle in February 1587.

When a king lost his head

468 **James VI and James I were the same man.** After Elizabeth I died, her distant cousin, James Stuart, became king of England and Wales. He was already king of Scotland, the sixth Scottish king called James, but the first in England with that name. He ruled each country separately – England and Scotland were not one united kingdom until 1707.

469 **James was the first anti-smoking campaigner.** Tobacco, which originated in America, was first brought to Europe in the late 16th century. It soon became popular but James hated it! He wrote a book describing smoking as 'a custom loathsome to the eye, hateful to the nose, harmful to the brain, and dangerous to the lungs'.

470 **James I was called 'the wisest fool'.** He was intelligent and ruled wisely, on the whole, from 1603 to 1625. But he did not look clever! His clothes were untidy and he slobbered and snivelled. He was also foolishly fond of several very silly friends.

471 **Charles I believed he had a divine right to rule.** King Charles (ruled 1625 to 1649) thought that kings were chosen by God. They had a divine (holy) right to lead armies and make laws. Anyone who disagreed with them was sinful. Not surprisingly, many of Charles's subjects did not share his views!

▶ A Cavalier (royalist) soldier (left) and a Roundhead soldier from Parliament's army.

◀ In 1653, Oliver Cromwell became Lord Protector. Here, Bible in hand, he makes a rousing speech to his Roundhead troops. Both sides in the English Civil War believed that they were fighting for God, and prayed that He would bring them victory.

472 **King Charles was a devoted husband and father and he was keen on the arts.** But he was not a very good king. He quarrelled so badly with Parliament about religion and taxes that he provoked a Civil War between Roundheads (supporters of Parliament) and Cavaliers (the royal family's supporters). After six years of fighting, from 1642 to 1648, Charles was put on trial, found guilty and executed.

473 **For eleven years, England (and Scotland and Wales) had no king.** At first, a Council of State ran the country. But in 1653 Parliament chose the commander of the Roundheads, Oliver Cromwell, to rule as Lord Protector. Cromwell was strict, solemn and deeply religious. He tried to bring peace. After his death in 1658 his son Richard ruled – badly. Parliament decided it was time for another king.

I DON'T BELIEVE IT!

Oliver Cromwell asked for his portrait to be painted showing him exactly as he was – even if it wasn't very attractive!

205

474 Charles II escaped to France when his father, Charles I, was killed. In 1660, he came back to England to be crowned king. Many people welcomed him. Like them, he wanted peace and religious toleration at home. Charles II enjoyed art, music, dancing and the theatre – and he had many girlfriends.

475 Charles was interested in all the latest scientific ideas. He set up a new Royal Observatory at Greenwich in south London, and appointed top astronomers to work there. Sadly, science killed him. His doctors gave him poisonous medicines and he died in 1685.

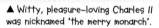
▲ Witty, pleasure-loving Charles II was nicknamed 'the merry monarch'.

476 Did James II try to pass off someone else's son as his own? When Charles died, his brother James became king. But James wanted to make England Catholic again. He had a daughter who had been brought up as a Protestant. Suddenly, and surprisingly, in 1688 James announced that his queen had given birth to a boy who would be England's next Catholic king. People accused James of smuggling a baby into the queen's bedroom. Parliament acted quickly – and turned James off the throne in 1688.

ROYAL QUIZ

1. What did Charles II set up at Greenwich?
2. Who was king after Charles II?
3. Who was Mary II's husband?
4. How did William III die?

Answers:
1. The Royal Observatory 2. James II
3. William of Orange
4. He was thrown off his horse when it tripped on a molehill

477 **Mary II was the daughter of King James II.** Unlike him, she was a Protestant, along with her husband, Dutch prince William of Orange. After sending James II into exile, Parliament asked Mary to be queen. She agreed, so long as her husband could be king as William III. They were crowned as joint monarchs in 1689.

▶ In 1688, Mary II and her husband William were called back to Britain from the Netherlands to become king and queen.

▶ Queen Anne warned her ministers not to bully her into making decisions, just because she was a woman.

478 **William III was killed by a mole!** One morning in 1702, William's horse tripped over a molehill and the king was thrown off. He died a few days later. Supporters of James II were delighted and hoped that James' son, James Edward Stuart, would become king. They praised the mole which had dug the molehill, calling him 'the little gentleman in black velvet'.

479 **Queen Anne united two kingdoms.** Anne was the younger sister of Mary II. Her private life was tragic. She became pregnant 17 times, but all her babies were either born dead, or died very young. But her reign (1702 to 1714) saw major changes in Britain. Parliament passed laws uniting England and Scotland and banning anyone but a Protestant from being the British king or queen.

Rulers from Germany

480 **George I never learned English!** He preferred to speak German or French. He also preferred living in Germany, where he ruled Hanover and other states as well England. George was the great-grandson of King James VI and I. He had the best claim to rule England after Queen Anne died without leaving any heirs.

▲ This coin was made in memory of the coronation of George I in 1714.

▼ George I was king of England, Wales and Scotland from 1714 to 1727.

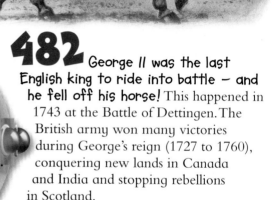

481 **George I kept his wife in prison.** George's wife, Sophia Dorothea, was lonely. When she made friends with a handsome nobleman, George was furious. He locked Sophia away in a German castle and refused to tell his children what had happened to their mother. They never forgave him.

I DON'T BELIEVE IT!

George II died while visiting the closet (royal lavatory). He collapsed there from a heart attack.

482 **George II was the last English king to ride into battle – and he fell off his horse!** This happened in 1743 at the Battle of Dettingen. The British army won many victories during George's reign (1727 to 1760), conquering new lands in Canada and India and stopping rebellions in Scotland.

483 James Edward Stuart was the only surviving son of King James II.

He lived in France, but claimed to be the rightful English and Scottish king. The British Parliament disagreed. They called James 'the Old Pretender'. In 1715 James invaded Scotland but he was forced out by George II's soldiers. He spent the rest of his life in Rome.

▲ Scottish highlanders, known as Jacobites, fought for James Edward Stuart and his son, Charlie.

▼ The Battle of Culloden in 1746 was the last major battle fought on British soil. Afterwards, Bonnie Prince Charlie spent many months in hiding, until Jacobite heroine, Flora MacDonald helped him to escape.

484 Bonnie Prince Charlie was called 'the Young Pretender'.

Charlie, who lived from 1720 to 1788, was the son of James Edward Stuart. He also claimed the right to be king. When he invaded Scotland in 1745 his attack went well. His army marched towards London but was forced to retreat by English soldiers. The next year, all that was left of Charlie's army was massacred at the Battle of Culloden, near Inverness.

The house of Hanover

485 **George III wanted to be a farmer.** George (ruled 1760 to 1820) lived during the Agricultural Revolution – a time when farmers were experimenting with new crops, techniques and machinery. George was most interested in these new developments. He liked to get away from London to countryside and talk to ordinary people.

▲ George III's long reign saw rebellions in America and Ireland, and a war with France.

486 **George III inherited a tragic disease.** In early life he was calm and sensible, but he had spells of mental illness throughout his last 60 years. While ill, he wore odd clothes, spoke to trees, mistook a pillow for his baby son and believed that the baby was dead.

487 **George IV was regent – deputy king – from 1811 to 1820 while his father George III was ill.** George (ruled 1820 to 1830) did not take his royal duties seriously. He lived for pleasure – eating, drinking, meeting friends and wearing the latest fashionable clothes.

▶ George IV was very interested in architecture and he paid for many fine new buildings, including the Royal Pavilion at Brighton.

488 William IV served in the Royal Navy — then sailed into a political storm. When he became king in 1830, ordinary people were demanding the right to vote. Parliament wanted to allow this, but William disagreed. After a long quarrel with Parliament, William was forced to change his mind, earning the nickname 'Silly Billy'.

I DON'T BELIEVE IT!

Due to his size, George IV earned the nickname 'Prince of Whales' when he was Prince Regent.

Victoria and Albert

489 **When Victoria became queen in 1837, many British people hated the monarchy.** They were shocked and disgusted by lazy, greedy kings like her uncle, George IV. Victoria promised to do better. She worked very hard at learning how to be queen, and took a keen interest in politics and the law for the whole of her life.

490 **Queen Victoria became 'the grandmother of Europe'.** In 1840 Victoria married her cousin, Prince Albert. They were very happy together and had nine children. Because Britain was so powerful, many other European countries wanted to show friendship. So they arranged marriages between Victoria's children and their own royal families. By the time Victoria died her descendants ruled in Germany, Russia, Sweden, Denmark, Spain, Greece, Romania, Yugoslavia – and Britain!

▼ Prince Albert always gave Queen Victoria wise advice, and encouraged British science, industry and the arts.

491
Victoria's Britain was 'the workshop of the world'. British engineers and businessmen were world leaders in technology and manufacturing. They invented steam-powered machines to mass-produce goods in factories and steam-powered ships and locomotives to transport them round the world. In 1851 Prince Albert organized the Great Exhibition in London to display goods made in 'the workshop of the world'.

492
Victoria – 'the Widow of Windsor' or 'Mrs Brown'? Prince Albert died in 1861, aged 42. Victoria was grief-stricken. She dressed in black as a sign of mourning until she died in 1901. For many years, the only person who could comfort her was a Scottish servant, John Brown. Some people said that Victoria had fallen in love with her servant and they secretly called her 'Mrs Brown'.

▲ The Great Exhibition of 1851 was held in a revolutionary new building – the Crystal Palace – made of iron and glass.

493
Queen Victoria ruled the largest empire in the world. It included most of the Indian subcontinent. Like many other British people, Victoria became fascinated by India's cultural heritage and rich civilization. She collected Indian jewels and art treasures and hired an Indian servant to teach her one of India's languages, Hindi.

ROYAL QUIZ
1. Who did Queen Victoria marry in 1840?
2. What did Prince Albert organize in 1851?
3. How many children did Queen Victoria have?
4. Who was John Brown?

Answers:
1. Prince Albert, her cousin
2. The Great Exhibition 3. Nine 4. Queen Victoria's servant and friend

Into the modern age

494 **Edward VII waited sixty years before he became king.** He spent a lot of his time, while waiting, having fun – he liked sailing, horse racing, gambling, fast cars and pretty women. But he also had a serious side. He spoke foreign languages very well and was a skilled politician and diplomat. After his mother, Queen Victoria, died, Edward reigned from 1901 to 1910.

◄ George V made the first royal Christmas broadcast to the people of Britain in 1932.

495 **George V changed his name.** Ever since Queen Victoria married Prince Albert, the British royal family had a German surname, Saxe-Coburg-Gotha. But in 1914 Britain and Germany went to war. So King George (ruled 1910 to 1936) changed his name to 'Windsor', the royal family's favourite home.

496 **Edward VIII said 'something must be done'!** In the 1920s and 1930s, Britain faced an economic crisis. Thousands of people lost their jobs. Edward felt sorry for them, and he visited poor communities. He caused a political row when he gave money to unemployed workers' families, and when he said that 'something must be done' by the government to help those out of work.

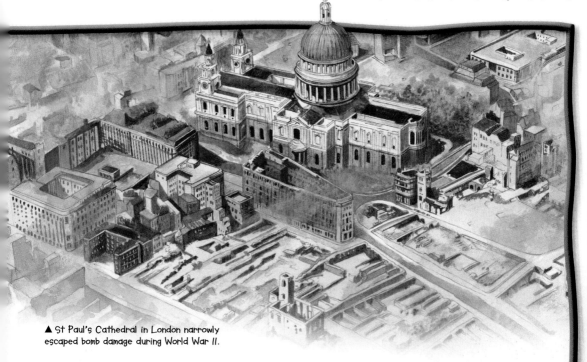

▲ St Paul's Cathedral in London narrowly escaped bomb damage during World War II.

497 **Edward VIII gave up his throne for love.** He became king in 1936 and immediately ran into trouble. He wanted to marry a divorced woman, Wallis Simpson, but the government, and the rest of the royal family, would not agree. So Edward abdicated (gave up the throne). He married Mrs Simpson, and spent the rest of his life living abroad.

I DON'T BELIEVE IT!

George V had the best stamp collection in the world.

498 **George VI never expected to be king.** But after Edward VIII abdicated he was next in line to the throne. George ruled from 1936 to 1952. Shy and with a stammer, George found royal duties difficult. People admired his devotion to duty and his settled family life.

499 **London was a dangerous place during World War II.** It was attacked by German warplanes. Many Londoners moved to the country but George VI and Queen Elizabeth, his wife, stayed in London to support the people, even after Buckingham Palace was bombed.

Queen Elizabeth II

500 **Elizabeth II has travelled farther than any other British monarch.** After 1950, many lands once ruled by Britain declared that they wanted to be independent. Queen Elizabeth respected this, but encouraged former British lands to stay in touch with the monarchy, and each other, by belonging to a new organization, called the Commonwealth. As head of the Commonwealth Queen Elizabeth has travelled thousands of miles meeting other Commonwealth leaders and peoples.

▶ Elizabeth II celebrated her Golden Jubilee (50 years as queen) in 2002 with parties, free concerts and a huge firework display.

Index

Index

Index

Acknowledgements

The publishers would like to thank the following sources for the use of their photographs:

t = top, b = bottom, l = left, r = right, c = centre

Page 134 Hulton Deutsch Collection/Corbis; 148(b) Columbia/Pictorial Press; 152 Pictorial Press; 153(l) Hulton Deutsch Collection/Corbis; 157(tr) Historical Picture Archives/Corbis, (bl) Pictorial Press; 158(cr) Paramount/Pictorial Press; 159(t) Rank/Pictorial Press; 166(tr) The Salvation Army International Heritage Centre, (bl) Pictorial Press; 170(b) Fotoware a.s 1997–2003; 172(b) The Art Archive/Eileen Tweedy; 174 Pictorial Press; 175(cl) Pictorial Press

All other photographs are from: Corel, digitalSTOCK, digitalvision, Fotolia.com, ImageState, iStockphoto.com, John Foxx, PhotoAlto, PhotoDisc, PhotoEssentials, PhotoPro, Stockbyte

The publishers would like to thank the following artists who contributed to this book:

Julie Banyard, Steve Caldwell, Peter Dennis, Nicholas Forder, Mike Foster, Terry Gabbey, Luigi Galante, Peter Gregory, Terry Grose, Gary Hincks, Sally Holmes, Richard Hook, John James, Angus McBride, Kevin Maddison, Janos Marffy, Alessandro Menchi, Andrea Morandi, Terry Riley, Pete Roberts, Martin Sanders, Peter Sarson, Mike Saunders, Rob Sheffield, Graham Sumner, Rudi Vizi, Steve Weston, Mike White

Cartoons by Mark Davis at Mackerel

All other artwork from the Miles Kelly Artwork Bank

Every effort has been made to acknowledge the source and copyright holder of each picture. Miles Kelly Publishing apologises for any unintentional errors or omissions.